T0158826

A Pilgrim on Peace Mountain

A Senior Woman's Survival at 9500 Feet

AMELIA ANDERS

WESTBOW
PRESS®
A DIVISION OF THOMAS NELSON
& ZONDERVAN

WestBow Press books may be ordered through booksellers or by contacting:

WestBow Press
A Division of Thomas Nelson & Zondervan
1663 Liberty Drive
Bloomington, IN 47403
www.westbowpress.com
1 (866) 928-1240

ISBN: 978-1-5127-7911-0 (sc)
ISBN: 978-1-5127-7912-7 (e)

Library of Congress Control Number: 2017903901

Print information available on the last page.

WestBow Press rev. date: 05/25/2017

The old trailer was a mess. The hollow core front door was broken with the bottom corner bent inward. Kitchen drawers were pulled out by an industrious pack rat which had moved in with energetic zeal. He had built his nest out of twigs and branches, dried leaves, screw drivers, jar lids, matches, can openers, spoons, and shreds of paper towels. A tinder box!

The pipes were rusted out. The wiring was chewed through by the pesky critters. Windows were cracked, and the first time I walked into the trailer, there, sitting on top of a pile of lumber in the back room was a squirrel. Part of the corrugated roof had blown off and wrapped itself around a Ponderosa pine. The trailer sat there on the side of the hill rocking in the wind.

And I was going to live in that?!

TABLE OF CONTENTS

Section 3   The End of the Roll

DEDICATION

This book is dedicated to every homeless person, every one of you who have had to leave home for any reason whether for poverty, joblessness, abuse, rape, rejection, beatings, slavery, divorce, lied about, unwanted pregnancy, hatred, life threatening danger, hunger, gang life, wars, religious beliefs. Maybe you never had a home. Perhaps there are no memories of a loving mother and father, a warm fire to gather around in the evening, sisters and brothers to play games with at night, no instruments to play to cheer the heart, no words of encouragement or hope. This book is dedicated to you.

I have not been through the full extent of all these things; I have only experienced a half dozen of them, and been homeless as you are, living in my car, eating out of a can, using restrooms in gas stations, temporarily renting spare bedrooms until my God brought me to a place where I could live in peace and He could take care of me.

The desire of His heart is to do the same for you. The desire of my heart is to tell you how He took care of me and loved me, grew me in His word, healed me of so many wounds, strengthened me and brought me back to an honorable life where I have had good jobs helping people, and now I own my own home and a Jeep and the side of a mountain where He taught me these lessons. If you read to the end, you will find out how God can help you do the same thing. He greatly loves you, He knows His plans for you and they are to bring you a future and a hope.

ACKNOWLEDGEMENTS

My sister Beth encouraged me to write about my adventures on the mountain. I would tell her about the wild dogs, or cooking on the woodstove, and she would say "Write it down." She has steadily kept me writing these last years to the finish, always encouraging. My son Mike has been in the background helping me with the technical things, getting the pen and ink drawings in order. My son Josh helped with contacts, myriad suggestions and not letting me give up. My daughter Ana has given me many useful hints down through the years. Thanks to my family and friends for your continual Godly support and wisdom.

INTRODUCTION

I had not planned to be a hermit. It was certainly not my highest goal in life and definitely not one to which my God had called me. (I was not the kind of hermit who sat in the doorway of a "wee stone hut." In fact, that would have been an improvement in my mode of shelter.) I was a senior citizen, the product of a phenomenon known as the fracturing of the family.

As a girl, I remember only one instance of a husband leaving his wife to disappear forever into the distant land of California. My mother, sister, and I visited the woman, taking her food and attempting to bring her hope. But she had no hope. I never heard what became of the woman. But the incident remained in the files of my girlhood mind. Divorce? We rarely heard of such a thing. Now seven decades later, it has, to our shame, become an everyday accepted part of our culture and I accept my part of the blame.

After living for thirty-six years with an angry, abusive man, my heart had died. My health had been going downhill for years. He refused to get help. I got counseling for quite a while but I didn't dare tell him.

I made the mistake of marrying a man who did not believe the same as I did and was not interested in God. The verbal abuse lasted throughout the marriage. The emotional, physical, financial, sexual, and spiritual abuse went underground when, five years into our marriage, he made a profession of faith in Jesus Christ. We joined a church and became active. He became a leader. Our life took on a split personality, one at church, one at work, another at home.

As time went by, I got counseling from various people. Back then, (we're talking fifty plus years ago) pastors were not trained in the knowledge and scriptural background, how to counsel in abusive situations. Some would say to abused women, "Go home, fix a nice dinner, and bake a pie for him. Then everything will be okay." But the woman would be right back in the pastor's office the next week, black and blue. In those days, if you were a Christian, you did not get a divorce. Not an option.

So my heart died. I no longer had the energy to handle the day-to-day scowls, the intimidating tone of voice, the put-downs. I wasn't good enough. I never would be. He was still "in love" with an old girlfriend of forty years ago.

Right.

As a young girl, I heard people arguing. But it never resulted in a family breaking up. When our family had guests and an occasional argument broke out, I would go outside and take a walk with one of my friends, waiting for things to calm down. My dad was always the peacemaker, quietly coming to the edge of the fray and speaking a gentle word or two, diffusing the situation. Today I see this precious gift of peacemaker in both my sons. This is amazing since they grew up in an abusive and violent household. Only the Spirit of the Lord can produce a quiet and gentle spirit. Both of them and my daughter have a strong faith in the Lord Jesus Christ. It's how we all survived.

As a result of abusive behavior, I began to realize I had to leave or succumb to increasingly poor health. I knew I would be on my own. A few people deserted me and felt sorry for him when I left. Because of the violent history, I had to leave without his knowledge while he was at work. I kept myself hidden in a safe place for some time. He found out where I was living. I had to threaten him with a restraining order to keep him away. I finally moved out of the area.

So follows the tale of my adventures on the side of a wild, rocky mountain, on my own again, determined to survive and put my trust in God who had kept us safe all those years.

<u>O Blackest Clouds</u>

O blackest clouds that boom and roll
Of evil does your thunder toll.
The glory that you try to hide
That lies beyond you in the skies
Shines through your noise and frightful night
I only see God's glory bright.
Through storm and plight one thought prevails,
I hear, O God, I've set my sails.

Amelia Anders, 1965

SECTION 1
The End of Innocence

"Better is a dry crust with peace and quiet than a house full of feasting with strife."
Prov. 17:1

CHAPTER 1

Vignette of a Girl

She was only eight years old, going on nine, but she ruled the woods. She knew every flower, vine, and tree by name. She knew the trails that crisscrossed over the hills and down to the Great Swamp Refuge beyond. The deer watched her. They were as used to her being in the woods as they were used to the squirrels, raccoons, red foxes, the myriad of birds, hawks, eagles, and the occasional dog.

The girl herself had no dog. She was always alone; her mother did not want her in the house. The house where the girl lived used to be a one-room schoolhouse, and before that it had been a stagecoach stop on the long haul between the east coast and points farther west. It was a house full of antique furniture and her mother kept it meticulously clean. It was no place for an adventurous girl.

Outside, the girl – an explorer at heart – kept busy. She constantly observed the sky and the clouds, and listened to the sounds of life in the woods. The woods behind her house became her outside home. The path up the hill led into her private domain. Her special time began when she climbed the hill and stepped into the forest.

On her daily walks, the girl always carried her walking stick. With it she overturned a rock while she watched an ant kingdom erupt from its tunnel to defend its domain. Satisfied, she gently lowered the rock and moved on down the deer trail toward her special place.

She built her lean-to after a hurricane had uprooted several tall trees. One of these, a sizeable walnut tree, fell with its branches wedged in those of an oak and a neighboring ash tree. The girl recognized the possibilities and gathered fallen branches from around the forest, propping them along the length of the fallen tree. Then she wove leafy branches and heavy wild grape vines over it all. Dried leaves formed the floor of her shelter and light rains didn't bother her.

Her lean-to was very acceptable for summer. However, for winter her shelter would be quite different.

Nearby there was an old cistern, at that time at least a hundred and thirty or forty years old, dug around the same time as the old stagecoach stop, to hold water for the horses and later for the one-room school house. A tired, still standing, rickety, creaking, windmill supplied the water. The woods had grown up around it and the girl might have been the only one who knew it was there. The girl came there whenever she could with an old rug, pillows and blankets, and a paper bag of butter and jelly crackers for her lunch.

Farther down the hill, through the trees and underbrush, the girl followed the almost overgrown deer trail to the edge of a meadow rich with tall grasses, wildflowers, herbs, butterflies, and birds. The girl stayed at the edge of the woods—watching, waiting. A hawk circled overhead, then gently slid down the currents of air toward the Great Swamp, cocking his head for some sign of a rabbit, a mouse, a shrew. Crickets chirped in the dark depths of the tall grasses. Spiders erected their finely engineered bridges from the top of one grassy seed head to another. Others already waited for their meals in the centers of their doily-shaped dinner tables.

A salamander worked its way out from under a rock and over to a small trickle of water that came from a tiny spring in some rocks at the edge of the meadow. The girl discovered the spring the year before. Since then, she hooked a metal drinking cup onto her belt and kept a penknife in her pocket, along with a magnifying glass, some safety pins, a kerchief, and Band-Aids.

The girl was aware of all the life around her.

She didn't move. Only her eyes drank in the living beauty as she breathed in the freshness of the moist earth and the breeze coming through the grasses that were as tall as she. She smiled. She was at home here—comfortable, content. Unknown to her, this was a foretaste of how her life would be decades later.

CHAPTER 2

Flashbacks

"It takes a great deal of time, effort, determination, planning and energy to avoid intimacy." (Amelia)

I stood in our motel living room where we were staying as we waited for our first house to be built. Suddenly two strong hands grabbed me from behind, flipped me around, grabbed me again by the upper arms and began shaking me back and forth. My husband's angry countenance spit out obscenities and accusations in my face. He shook me and shook me, each motion as bad as a whiplash, my neck arching in pain over and over. I lost track of how long this lasted—minutes certainly, but it seemed like days. The effects lasted for years. When it stopped I was disoriented … dizzy … trying to understand what had just happened and why, my feelings for him utterly slammed into the dirt, my heart shredded.

My mind whirled. I couldn't focus on the things he said. I stumbled away from him into our bedroom and collapsed on the bed. My neck hurt, my shoulders ached, my legs were shaky. I had no energy except to lie there and try to suppress my sobs. I pulled the covers up but couldn't sleep, wondering if when he came to bed this was going to happen again. A sickening realization, a certainty grew within me and I knew I would never be safe in my own home again.

I cried out! I sobbed for God to help me, to stop him! I was six months pregnant with our daughter. God! She had to be all right! Father, help her, this little one, this dear child. Don't let her be hurt! Comfort her, comfort me! You are our only hope.

I stirred myself. I had to get out of this place! The covers were wrapped around my neck and I was gasping for air. God, help! I woke up crying out in anguish, thrashing the pillow. I sat up sweat drenched in the dark. Where was I?

Oh.

Yes.

I was having another flashback. They were getting worse. Several times a week I would wake up in fear and disorientation, remembering another incident as clearly as if it had just happened, crying out for help.

Back in the fifties, there was no help. There were no safe houses, no shelters, nowhere to go. Besides, I'm a Christian. This doesn't happen to nice respectable people. Who would believe me?

"What did you do to make him behave that way?"

"You've got to be a better wife."

"Either quit complaining or leave!"

And go where?

It happened again shortly after we moved into our new home. My husband pounded down the hall in a rage into the living room, yelling at top volume, giving me no time to respond. He grabbed the car keys, walked out the door, and sped away in the car.

As I sat there trying to process his outburst, I made a decision. I was not going to be there when he came back. I packed a suitcase full of diapers for our son Mike, who was almost two, left the house by the back door, threw the suitcase over the back fence and helped him climb over into the next yard. We went through the yard, across two streets and to the main road. We just started walking. I was headed for a friend's house where I thought we would be safe. A police car stopped and gave us a ride to the closest intersection where we could walk to my friend's house.

My friend and her husband welcomed us, but could tell I was upset. Conversation was stilted as I was not sure how much to tell them. By then I was about seven and a half months pregnant. I needed a place of safety. Suddenly the phone rang. The husband answered it. "Yes, she's here." It was him! The husband put the phone down and told me, "Your husband will be here in about ten minutes."

"No!" I gasped. My discomfort was obvious. I felt betrayed. I found out later that he had called around to various friends to see where I was.

When he arrived, he had obviously cleaned up and changed his clothes. He was very calm and pleasant. The two men spoke for a few minutes and then my husband said we needed to leave.

In the car on the way home he turned to me and with venom in his voice he said: "Don't you ever do this to me again!" Do this to him? I had done something to him? Now I had to be very careful until my daughter was born. I would be quiet. I would be extremely good.

CHAPTER 3

Summarily Dismissed

After living for thirty-six years with an angry, abusive man, the heart gives out. My health had been sliding downhill with a growing number of symptoms for a while. I found there are certain telltale symptoms that develop in an abused woman, which I began to notice in other women besides myself. Sitting in my doctor's office one day, I overheard another woman talking about the same symptoms that I had. The same group of symptoms are involved: the faulty metabolism of sugar known as hypoglycemia; low sex drive; weight gain around the middle; early graying of hair and falling hair; PMS; thyroid problems; allergies; digestive problems; constipation. The big thing for many women is early menopause. These problems are not the kind that make it impossible to go to work but might increase sick days, lack of energy, lower motivation. I had the added diagnosis of skin cancer and exhausted adrenal glands. This resulted in a general lack of energy, listlessness, and purposelessness. My doctor had given me adrenal cortex extract shots and tablets to maintain health. This did help my energy level.

I was a certified, licensed massage therapist, so I tried to take good care of myself. On the days I worked, I did six, seven, eight hours of massage. I bought a juicer and made fresh carrot-celery juice, adding fresh herbs and lemon. Sometimes I made my own multi-vegetable drink. I taught natural-food cooking classes, so I knew how to grind grain, bake whole-grain bread, and make pizzas, soups, salad dressings, and yogurt from scratch. I served healthy meals at home with as many fresh vegetables as possible. I was doing my best to stay healthy, but the constant abuse became too much for me.

My husband refused to get help. I made the mistake of marrying a man who did not know the Lord and was not the least interested in Him. His subtle and not-so-subtle verbal abuse lasted throughout the marriage. There was emotional abuse making fun of my art work; mocking the goals of my relationship with God (Job 31:10-31); physical abuse; mental abuse (telling me what I really thought or meant); financial abuse (not wanting me to have my own bank account, not willing to provide warm coats and boots for winter); sexual abuse; and spiritual abuse (using the

Word of God against me, which went underground when, five years into the marriage, he made a profession of faith in Christ). We joined a church and became very active. He became a leader. Our life took on a split personality. He had one personality at church, another at work, another at home.

"I'll love you if you're good!" he would say; but could we ever be good enough? Could love, tenderness, understanding ever be a part of our lives? Or was love a weakness that couldn't be allowed? And we must be "good" in church too, so no one would be embarrassed. .

The statement I made at the beginning of chapter 2 appears to be true with many people who have to be in control instead of allowing God to be in control.

I got counseling from various people down through the years. Sadly, pastors back then were lacking in the knowledge and scriptural background of how to counsel in this generational onslaught of abusive cases. There is rarely just a one time "oops" in a relationship where correcting things and being sorry ends all future violence. A profession of faith in Jesus doesn't stomp out the deep seeds of bitterness and rage. An entirely new generation of people have lived and grown and survived through the pain of devastated lives. These are the people who have said, "Enough!" and run out the doors of their homes, not putting up with the pain any more, gathering up their children, taking them to safe places that have been created because of the need. These are the ones who, with determination, have created the safe houses for our future generations. Now there are many places people can go and receive help, counseling not condemnation, hope not rejection, eat food in peace without angry words, and sleep knowing their children will be safe. Thank you, every one of you.

I knew, as I was raising my children, that if we left, he would eventually find us and there would be hell to pay. I knew this from experience. With no known places of safety back then, I made the decision to stick it out and make sure my children were taken care of to the best of my ability.

The end came during our last vacation down the West Coast. I had saved my allowance and bought some new clothes: swimsuits, blouses, a couple of skirts, and shoes. My husband loved to have me model the clothes he had bought for me.

One day in the motel he handed me a package and told me to open it. Inside were several dresses and other articles of women's clothing. As I tried them on, I noticed they were not new. "I got them at Goodwill," he said. The colors were dull, brown, and worn with hanging threads. I started crying. I took the clothes off, wadded them into a pile and threw them at him. I told him to take them back.

Another evening was supposed to be special. He made reservations at a lovely old restaurant on the coast. I dressed carefully in my new clothes and I knew I looked good. He thought so, too.

As we entered the restaurant, the atmosphere was elegant with subdued lighting, linen tablecloths, napkins and crystal candlesticks on every table. Fresh flowers were in crystal vases. Waves of soft music sang to us. As we were seated, crystal glasses were filled with iced lemon water. China plates with paper doilies were ready for appetizers. How nice. I was going to enjoy this evening!

Our salad and fresh seafood arrived and then dessert. When we were almost finished, he paused and asked me a question.

"Did I ever tell you what I was going to do after you die?"

I put my fork down and stared at him. It took me a minute to process his question because, at fifty-eight, I was still in reasonably good health, comparatively speaking. I wasn't using a cane or walker to get around. I hadn't been diagnosed with end-stage cancer or serious heart problems. I was an active massage therapist holding down a physically demanding job.

"No, you didn't," I finally responded. I didn't want to know what he was going to do. It had not been uppermost in my mind.

Clearing his throat again and rearranging the silverware on the table, he said, "Right after the funeral, I'm going to talk to your best friend, Cheryl, tell her to divorce her husband, and ask her to marry me."

Clunk!

My digestive juices coagulated in my stomach; the meal, the evening, the vacation were ruined along with any hopes for the future.

I was not blind. I knew he had been attracted to her, but he was drawn to any attractive woman who also had a good education and might provide a good income. So …

I had just received the ultimate put-down. A verbal, public "divorce" in a place that didn't encourage any display of anger, certainly not the two glasses of ice water I should have dumped in his lap!

I was stunned at his cruelty! I put my napkin down and sat, shaken, on the edge of the chair while he paid the bill. It was over. This farce of a marriage was over. Not only was my husband planning my funeral, he was planning who he was going to spend his life with after the formalities of the funeral were over.

He stayed in California and I flew home. He said he had another week of "work" there. Upon arriving home I began making quiet arrangements to leave. The children were grown and gone. Thirty-six years of this kind of treatment was enough! Over the next few months I moved out of the master bedroom, stepped up my counseling, made sure my car was in good working order, located another out-of-the-way place to live when the time came, and stayed very quiet. And I waited.

When he got back from his trip he placed his suitcase on the living room floor, opened it and took out a rolled up poster. Taking it into his office he unrolled it and push pinned it to the wall. It was a picture of Hawaii. He hadn't been "working." He had gone to Hawaii. For years he spoke to me about going to Hawaii. After this, he never mentioned it again.

CHAPTER 4

Come Away, My Beloved

Finally the time arrived when I could go. Over the last few months I had begun to develop an ulcer. The longer I stayed, the more cruel his remarks became. He had stopped wearing his wedding ring months before. Men know how to get rid of a woman without asking for a divorce. And then they can say, "Well, she wanted to leave." You bet I did!

I had gone away for the weekend. I stayed away until Monday morning, sitting in my car down the street, waiting until after he had gone to work. After he left, I entered the house and called some friends to bring a rental truck to the house. I grabbed a pad of sticky notes and went through the house labeling each piece of furniture that was mine, all the antiques that I had inherited from my parents, and other personal items. I quickly packed my clothes and was ready when the truck arrived. Four young men piled out and I gave directions. Two and a half hours later all my things were loaded and the truck left.

I went to the abuse center and filled out papers. I appeared before a judge and received a restraining order. The judge asked me if I had filed for a divorce yet. I said no. She told me I needed to do so as quickly as possible.

After court, I went back to the house and cleaned it from top to bottom, rearranging the furniture to make it presentable. I left him a handwritten letter telling him goodbye, along with ample reasons for leaving. He later denied ever getting this letter.

When I received the restraining order, I was asked if he had any weapons. I said yes, that he kept a knife on the floorboard of his car, another in the top drawer of his nightstand and a Swiss army knife in his pocket. He kept a knife in his suitcase when he traveled. He had to surrender it to the pilot on a trip we took to Europe once. (This was the late 80s.)

As I left the house for the last time, I knew I was not just leaving him. I was leaving security, the shelter of a home, and health insurance, and walking into loneliness, hunger, rejection of friends and children, and the puzzlement of family members. I placed myself in isolation and safety for a few months where no one could find me. I had to. He did try to find me. It took him a few months. I had to move again.

After the divorce proceedings began, my lawyer informed me that, when reviewing my husband's financial records, it was discovered he had been spending a thousand to fifteen hundred dollars on himself every month just like clockwork for at least the last five years. No records were available before that. The money just vanished from the account. It was never deposited. This amounted to about seventy-five thousand dollars!

I know what you may be thinking. The same thoughts went through my mind. *What did he do with it?* Someday I will know. It has been almost fifteen years since he passed away. Just know I am free and I have forgiven. The Bible is clear and what some men don't understand is that women run on love. Even after forgiveness, there is still the puzzling pain of a lost, unredeemable marriage which could have, should have been so different, with a little bit of love. Men put high test gas in their cars for performance. Try a little high test love with your wife, and watch out! Women take whatever men give them and multiply it. Sex equals a baby. A house equals furniture. Food money equals dinner on the table. A fight equals anger, pain. Adultery equals incredible loss.

CHAPTER 5

On Thin Air

There is a time under heaven to do what is right. There is a time to end abuse and to start healing. There is a time to start living and loving life again. The time to cry is over and the time to laugh is just beginning.

I've made lists below of the advantages and disadvantages of leaving. I think they are important to review at this point, lest you think I just mindlessly stayed as long as I did. It is also good to review my thoughts and reasoning as I look back over this part of my life.

Some of the advantages of staying were the relative security of having a roof over my head, a place of safety from robbers and mockers, health insurance, church friends, (this was true as long as none of them knew about the abuse), a social life, established patterns, credit, sleeping in a warm bed, a warm house and food, and children pretty much unaware of conditions between their parents because they were no longer living at home. It may seem strange that I mention these simple things that many today take for granted. But as I look around at the growing number of homeless people and whole families out on the street, I realize there are many people who don't have this choice. I knew what I was doing in leaving these things. To homeless people, I say that I have been where you are.

The disadvantages of staying were constant fear, anger, violence, continually being threatened with money being taken away, even the money I earned. Even though he made good money, he wanted me to buy my clothing at recycle shops. He asked me to sell my antiques and other furniture that I'd inherited from my parents to get money for him. I didn't. He refused to pay back my inheritance he "borrowed." Like I mentioned previously, he gave me a mother's day present purchased at a recycle shop, (six articles of other women's used clothing). What an insult! Did I mention that he threw out most of my good dresses? Or maybe he recycled them. When we got married I had some very nice clothes. They would just disappear one by one from my closet, one here another there And then he sent me to buy a used sewing machine so I could make my own clothes. I did.

The advantages of leaving were that I had God and I trusted Him, I had my own car (paid for), I had a job, a certificate of deposit, and my mountain property with an abandoned trailer on it. I had been a Girl Scout, so I knew I could survive. I could live by myself and figure things out. I was teachable. I could live quietly, eat simple food, and live on very little. I could buy firewood to burn in my woodstove and oil for my lamps at night.

The disadvantages of leaving were that I had no steady jobs, just seasonal ones, as a fully trained, certified and licensed massage therapist. I also had one year of college and one year of art school but uncertainty in many areas.

The consequences of leaving were that I had no permanent home, no insurance (as I was not old enough for Medicare), little safety, and no social life. I was abandoned by acquaintances and criticized by people. They told me I shouldn't leave, that this could be fixed. (Should I live as a divorced woman in my own home? Many women do.) Talk about denial! Things just can't be like everyone else thinks they should be.

I experienced broken relationships. My children were hurt by my leaving. It took years to go through healing in these areas. Mostly it takes forgiveness. I was very thankful that both my parents had gone home to be with the Lord.

The things I learned after I left are what few other people would be willing to learn. I learned that I could trust God to supply all my needs according to His riches in glory by Christ Jesus. I learned to listen to Him. The Holy Spirit would speak to me through the Word. The Word gave me peace at night when wild animals were just outside my door. The Word held my world together when the storms raged and the wind blew outside and I had no lightning rods. When I asked God to send His angels to patrol my property and my long driveway and keep unscrupulous strangers and thoughtless hunters off my property, I had a confidence that He did it.

I learned that my needs were different from my wants. I learned that some things are just not important. TV was not important; music was. Running water wasn't important; having water to drink at all, was. Central heat was not important; having enough wood for my woodstove was. Having electricity was not important; having enough oil to be able to read and write by oil lamps at night was. Cooking on modern, up-to-date appliances was not important; being able to cook at all, on my woodstove, was. Being able to keep my food fresh in an electric refrigerator was not important; being able to get ice three times a week was. Being a couple of blocks from the nearest store wasn't important; planning ahead for my needs was. Being fifty or a hundred miles away from church wasn't important; I would drive as far as necessary to be with those who loved Him too.

My mountain neighbors were helpful. Many bore the fruit of kindness that was refreshing. (A divorced woman back then carried shame and a bad name in some communities.) I have to admit that this has changed remarkably in the last two or three decades. Now there are many groups available to help and give direction and shelter to those of us who are unwanted.

I found I didn't need a lot of friends and I certainly didn't need fair-weather friends or curiosity seekers. I didn't like to be used and I didn't need to be "fixed" by somebody else. That's God's job.

I also learned that nothing is safe if someone else wants it. I learned not to trust just anyone who wanted to help. I learned how to protect myself and that I could learn to do many things myself. It was worth going through hardship, living by myself, to have peace. It was worth doing without to have a quiet home. I learned that quality time is better than quantity time. I could do without TV. Wow!

I had to find new patterns, establish new credit, and deal with gossip and manipulations. Many times I would find myself sleeping in my car, parked in front of a friend's house, eating out of a can, trying to stay warm, careful to wake before daylight and leave before the family woke up. I used bathrooms at gas stations to get cleaned up. I was too young for Social Security, so I knew I'd have to sink or swim myself. At first there was the fear that my former husband would find me and force me to come back as he did before. But I realized my trust was in God, not in what might happen.

I learned to buy quality tools and not to loan them out, but to go with my tools to help others and bring my tools back home again. I learned how to barter. It seems to be the mountain way. I would be afraid but my trust would be in God. I learned there are good, helpful people in this world and there is no need to be violent or abusive.

To deal with my pain I had to make decisions about my life that said pain and loss of love don't matter because this couldn't be an emotional decision. I had to say to myself,, "It doesn't matter if this hurts. It doesn't matter if my heart is broken. I'm sorry if this decision hurts my children but they are no longer living under this barrage of hate."

Hope is essential to survival. Faith and emotional health require drastic action in a time of irreconcilable situations. My past failure to leave him might have made me afraid to try again. But I had to use my common sense and base my decisions on what I knew I had to do at that point. I had this inner sense, a knowing, that if I continued to stay in this broken relationship, I would not be alive in another couple of years.

The Word of God was hidden in my heart. I reviewed the Old and New Testaments. Malachi 2:16 says "'I hate divorce,' says the LORD God of Israel, 'and I hate a man's covering himself [or his wife] with violence as well as with his garment,' says the LORD Almighty" (added words from a footnote in NIV 1984). All these things I was willing to give up in order to place my life entirely in God's hands.

And I did. The world was not easy on me. I was robbed a number of times. Once two young men literally crashed down a couple of doors to get into the house to rob all of us. I moved seven times in one year. I got jobs that turned out to be temporary. I rented extra bedrooms from friends. I lived in many basements. I bought food to cook meals and bake bread for the families with whom I stayed. Eventually, it became more and more clear that I had another important decision to make.

I did what I had to do, go someplace where I could live in peace, a place where no one else would want to come and no one could force me to leave. When my mountain called my name, I went up to my wild property and lived—on thin air.

But I lived.

SECTION 2

The Pilgrimage

"Blessed are those whose strength is in you, who have set their hearts on pilgrimage."
Psalm 84:5

CHAPTER 6

Peace for Sale

When one lives alone on the side of a remote mountain—with no artificial sounds, no music, no one to talk to—the ears become very sensitive. The humdrum of busy streets, car horns, passersby talking, someone on a cell phone, sales clerks, grocery carts, kids running—all of these things people are accustomed to in their normal urban lives—disappear. All of a sudden the mind can rest. The ears stop ringing. The need to hasten isn't there.

Imagine yourself on the mountain. A new thought hits your awareness. Isn't life supposed to be like this? You feel your emotions and your blood pressure letting down, your muscles relaxing and your headache fading away. You take a deep breath because something is missing—the smell of civilization, the exhaust of cars, smoke from industries, tobacco smoke. However there is one familiar smell that occasionally wafts across your senses—wood smoke. Someone has built a fire in their fireplace. Memories come back of campfires, marshmallows, s'mores, the sizzle of hot dogs and hamburgers, sauerkraut and mustard and a friend playing a guitar. Someone's telling jokes or creepy stories. Laughter.

You breathe in the sweet air and relive the memories, along with the aroma of the pine trees and the sage. You catch a glimpse of a golden eagle sailing on the currents along the mountain. His mate circles just below. They call to each other. A couple of indigo buntings fly up from their nest. You turn to the east and a rocky hilltop beckons. As you climb your body realizes you are breathing thinner air. As you reach your goal, your eyes can do something they've not done in a long, long time—see forever. Clouds seventy-five miles away carry rain to a distant valley. You look up to see a rainbow forming in the stream of clouds passing over the sun. A breeze has come all the way around the world to greet you, whispering of how life could be if you lived up here. A rock right on top is a perfect spot to rest. Yes. When was the last time you thought about just resting?

A squirrel scampers away. You sit. How far can your eye travel? Mountains fifty, seventy, a hundred miles away wait for you to identify them. You wonder if someone on that far mountain is looking your way, trying to guess the name of your mountain. It's Peace. You shade your eyes and call out to the other mountains: "It's Peace, Peace Mountain!" The warm sun snuggles into your shoulders. You open a bottle and let the cold water trickle down your throat. A large bumblebee investigates the berry bushes nearby.

Something inside you turns over. Dizziness hits you. You go through a paradigm shift. You've found something you didn't know you were looking for. A swirling battle is going on within. You just got here and now you don't want to go home.

Home. Where is it? That's that place where you have to go. It's that suddenly noisy, busy place that used to be normal. Up at six or earlier, out the door by seven. Got to get to work by … The report must be ready … They're depending on you …

The squirrel comes out again and stares at you. He digs for a buried tidbit then moves down the hill. You sit there smiling a foolish smile. What if …? What if you built a little cabin just over there by those trees or near that rock outcropping? What would it take? Your mind starts working, but this time it's creating, dreaming. You could sit out here on the porch in the evening and watch the stars. Up here you could see the shooting stars, the constellations—Orion, the Big Dipper, the Pleiades, the North Star. You could set up your telescope right over there! You could watch the sun come up. Your kids, your grandkids could camp in the front. Why, they could build a tree house over in that large ponderosa! You'd help them... What … are … you … thinking!? Are you insane?

It's too late. Peace has stolen your heart.

That's what happened to my husband and me forty-five years ago. He decided to take one of our vacations and find a piece of property in the Colorado Mountains. We rejected several places.

One rancher seemed to know what we wanted. He drove us up into the higher elevations where he had thirty-five-acre and larger tracts of land. Up and up we traveled following a tiny stream that broadened out and then seemed to disappear altogether in the gravelly soil only to reappear sparkling and shining as if to encourage us as we went along. Cattle grazed by the road that had turned to dirt a mile off the main highway. The smell of wild sage wafted into the windows. Donkeys grazed in fields along with the horses and cows. Higher up deer browsed right near the stream. They looked up at us but didn't run. I wondered if this place was some kind of Eden.

As we curved around a mountain, twisting up a rise into a high mountain valley, antelope grazed on the slopes among the hills. A mother bear and her cub browsed along a stream a thousand feet away, her head up watching us. The higher we drove, the deeper blue became the sky. The rancher turned up an almost invisible track and crept up a steep hill, wound around another until he stopped—at the top of the world! My husband was excited as he got out of the jeep. He walked over to the rocky outcropping, placed his hands on his hips, and stood staring at the unending vista—snow-capped mountains to the west and more to the east, a long, wide valley to the south disappearing into haze barely revealing the Spanish Peaks. A white teepee with its poles thrust itself up through some tall ponderosas down the valley. Had we actually stepped back in time?

"Looks like we just bought ourselves a piece of property!" he said. "Come on! Let's walk down the hill." His eyes took it all in. I could see the wheels spinning. "Look, the house could go right here against this south-facing slope. The hill will break the north winds. This will be the perfect spot for a solar home. I'll talk to the rancher and see if he can improve the road and swing it around here with a circle drive." He stood there with a smile of satisfaction on his face as he figured it all out. It was an outstanding spot. We both loved it and we hadn't yet seen all of it.

That night, after the land was ours, my husband built a fireplace in a small copse of trees near the top and our first meal was simple: hamburgers, baked beans, bannock bread, and hot chocolate. With full stomachs, our whole family camped on the top in sleeping bags. None of us could sleep as the heavens hung right down, sparkling and floating over our dreams. There was no moon, so every planet and constellation stood out. Shooting stars sailed by. Quiet night sounds finally lulled us to sleep, the night hawk making his tour over the area. The magic and the peace had worked.

As I drifted off to sleep, thoughts whirled in my head. This must be God's backyard, the very edge of His footstool. Did I hear angels singing us to sleep, patrolling our camp ground? What a display of God's glory!

In the morning the huge valley was filled with mist, miles wide and forever long, sparkling in the peachy red sunrise that gives the name to the Sangre de Christo Mountains (Spanish for "Blood of Christ").

As you drive along looking for your own place, remember, you won't find it; it will find you. It is calling your name. You won't realize till you're there and look around sensing the peace and the beauty and you'll ask yourself, "Didn't I see a 'For Sale' sign down below? I've got to check on the way back. There must be one!" You'll make a call tomorrow. No. Tonight! As soon as you can reach a phone!

Yep.

What would you give for peace?

CHAPTER 7

Surviving

Living on the side of a rugged mountain in a tired, dilapidated trailer by myself, I knew fear and loneliness, two neighbors who tried to get in on a regular basis.

One night as I was sitting on my couch reading by one of the oil lamps, there was the first indication of a problem. It was about nine thirty in the evening, a time I always looked forward to, when I could relax after the chores of the day were finished. All at once the cats went crazy. They jumped onto the back of the couch, pushed the curtains aside, and stared outside—watching something. They made funny little mewling sounds and held their mouths open panting in fear. If that isn't enough to curl hair on the back of your neck, I don't know what is!

I had prepared for this moment.

As the object of their fear moved around the trailer, the cats followed, jumping up on the kitchen counter to watch. They then careened to the opposite side of the trailer, scrambled to the top of the bookcase and visually tracked it, their tails straight up like bottle brushes, their claws dug in. I knew it wasn't the male cat that had been courting my spayed female (dummy!). He yowled as he prowled. It wasn't a coyote because there was no arrogant yapping. This animal was very quiet ... until he climbed up on my deck. Instantly the cats were pinned by their claws to the back of the couch again looking through the curtains at the deck.

With no utilities including electricity, I couldn't just snap on a spotlight to light the yard and see our intruder. As a precaution, I got out my shotgun and laid it down on the coffee table in front of the couch, placing the box of shells next to it, and waited. With my rechargeable million-candle-power flashlight, I carefully looked through the curtains and saw our guest. A four-hundred-plus-pound bear, a rogue with two yellow tags in his ear, was estimating his chances of dinner being served on the deck. Since the restaurant was closed for the night, I sat back down, held my shotgun ready and waited for him to leave.

No, I was not about to open the door and face this bruin, even with a shotgun at three feet! I'd had a steel door installed earlier for just this reason. I did not want to upset him the least little bit or he would have come right through the door or a window. Six years previously, a hungry, mad bear had killed a neighbor five miles away as the eagle flies. They found parts of him a day or two later and a bullet hole through the front door of his trailer. He had apparently been sleeping on his roof. He had been careless, feeding his dogs outside and throwing his garbage out the door. He was only about twenty-two years old. Wildlife Management did come and cart away a bear shortly thereafter.

By that time I did have a phone so I decided to call my nearest neighbor. No answer. The people in my nine-thousand-foot-high mountain valley go to bed early. I tried to read. Hah! My hands were sweaty and shaking. My stomach did a strange spastic dance. I prayed. I called some friends in the city who I knew would still be awake. They had company—their in-laws. When I relayed my problem, they responded, "Don't put out the honey pot!" I laughed and hung up the phone. Hopefully Bruno would go away when he ceased to attract any more attention. In a while, the cats calmed down and I guessed the bear must have moved on. I went to bed … sort of, keeping my clothes on and keeping the gun handy and tried to sleep. I asked the Lord to send His angels to patrol my yard and to keep any more large animals away for the rest of the night. The next morning he was gone, probably begging for food from one of my other neighbors. Good! I had a potato salad to make and a Fourth of July picnic to attend.

As a single woman again, I was driven by the need to survive when my former husband refused to pay any more maintenance. He warned me with these words: "Don't ask! Don't even think of asking for any more money!" As part of the divorce settlement I had received the thirty-five-acre tract of land we'd bought years ago. I had not been old enough to get on Social Security and had reached the point where I had thirty-five cents in my coin purse. An old trailer had been abandoned on the property fifteen years before.

The land was raw and rugged, no improvements, no utilities anywhere in the high mountain valley. There were almost twenty miles of dirt road between me and civilization. No power. No water. No phones until recently. No gas stations. No streetlights. Just quiet, open, wonderfully deep blue sky, snow-iced mountain peaks, the cry of the golden eagle, the presence of God and me.

It was certainly a dangerous chance I was taking, living alone on the side of a mountain, but when a person is desperate, it sparks determination, which brings forth a courage I didn't realize I had until I found myself sitting in my car with the sun falling down through the sky, no money in my pocket and a mountain calling my name. True, living on my property was living at a lower level even than welfare. At least welfare would have given me a few rooms with lights, running water, a warm dry place to sleep, TV, a small kitchen, maybe a yard. Had I made that decision, I would have missed the adventure of my life! After all, even at sixty plus I was an old scout, wasn't I?

God can use even a senior citizen to accomplish His purposes. What? Oh, my. Look at Moses who freed the children of Israel at eighty. Look at Sarah who bore Isaac at ninety and died at 127. Noah built the ark between the ages of five and six hundred years. Joshua just got started in his military career at sixty, after walking in the desert with Moses and Caleb from the age of twenty, for forty years and he was a strong powerful warrior and leader. Joseph became prime minister of Egypt at thirty, after serving a prison sentence, saving the whole known world at that time from starvation and died at the age of 110. No wonder the Bible tells us to honor the gray-haired man or woman! We're just getting started! And we know how to listen to and obey the Word of the Lord. Not that we always do, but we do know.

CHAPTER 8

Homesteading

My mountain land is above nine thousand feet in the Rocky Mountains of Colorado. This land had been owned by our family for over twenty-eight years. As a single woman again, I knew it wouldn't be an easy task to start over, but as an old scout I wouldn't be giving up easily. There was no well, no improvements. My closest neighbor was over half a mile away. Quite remote. Still … the land drew me. It had called to me from every city and town in which we'd lived over the years. Now my own adventure in homesteading began.

Years ago, homesteading was used to settle large, remote, newly opened sections of public land in this country. With the Homestead Act of 1862, any person age twenty-one or over or who was the head of a family might acquire ownership of a tract of 160 acres or less of public land without cost, if they lived on the land and cultivated it for five years. Or if they had the cash, they could buy the land for the sum of $1.25 per acre. Later the free homestead sites were increased to 340 acres, and in 1916 to 640 acres. That's one square mile! During that time people would dig a well, plant a garden, build a house and barn, raise cattle and chickens, harvest and sell what they grew, and become self-supporting. If they succeeded, they kept the land free except for the payment of administrative fees. Only in America!

Homesteads were built with time, effort, sweat, and determination. Now I wondered if I had what it would take. I had two things going for me. First, I already owned the land, and second, an old trailer was on the land. Almost forty years old, it sat on the brow of the hill, rocking in the wind. Part of the old corrugated roof had blown off, curling itself around a nearby ponderosa pine. Nevertheless, it was shelter.

I bartered with a neighbor who owned heavy equipment to put in a quarter-mile driveway past the trailer down into a sheltered glen. With his bulldozer he towed the trailer along the new drive into the glen to rest next to a dry stream bed. We leveled it with jacks, setting it on concrete blocks and two-by-fours for permanent support.

At that time in my high mountain valley, since there were no utilities, I couldn't just pull the trailer up and plug it in. After the trailer was leveled, I cleaned out the inside and made it livable. Over the next few months, I replaced the broken front door with a new steel door and added a wooden deck with steps made from used lumber. My youngest son Josh climbed up on the roof and "mudded" it with asphalt for waterproofing. He helped me by rebuilding the kitchen floor and covering it with new vinyl. We tore out the old carpet and put down used jade-green carpet, painted the dark paneling and ceilings white, and replaced the old fifties wall covering with drywall and green floral wallpaper. Broken windows were re-glazed, leaks stopped, mouse holes closed up with tin can lids, and cabinets cleaned out and disinfected after the eviction of an industrious and persistent pack rat.

I had no well, so I carried my water in twice a week from various neighbors' wells. The closest electricity was about three and a half miles away. For the cost of twenty-five thousand dollars per mile to bring in new power, I could burn a lot of lamp oil, not to mention drilling a well, erecting a solar system and installing a septic system. Bringing power onto my land would cost seventeen to eighteen thousand dollars, just from the road! Besides, an excellent solar system that could run everything in my home—TV, computers, lights, garage door opener, kitchen appliances, shop tools—would cost about ten to twelve thousand dollars back then. No contest. Most of my neighbors had 12-volt solar electric systems with inverters; wells; propane tanks that ran stoves, refrigerators, and water heaters; gas furnaces; and a few had electric wind generators. Wind generators can take the strain off solar systems during high usage and during long storms when the sun is covered with clouds. They also generate power day or night whenever a breeze is blowing. Since it only requires a wind speed of about seven miles an hour to move the blades, this is no problem here in Colorado. Barring storms, the average wind speed is between five to ten miles an hour. I personally would come to appreciate this as I read late and sometimes write into the wee hours of the morning. At this time I had no such luxury as electricity and did my reading and writing by oil lamps. (Yes, I wrote with a pen on a legal pad.) One oil lamp is not enough light and two would be cumbersome on an end table so I "shaded" my lamps with large sheets of aluminum foil, one long edge tucked into the top of the chimney to reflect more light, the two ends spread outward like silver wings. It works.

CHAPTER 9

Communications

Imagine a place with no phones, no telephone poles or cell phone towers, no TV, no underground utilities, no water, no gas, no house-to-house communication. Imagine just wide open, unencumbered air; peace and quiet to be sure. That's one reason I loved my place with acres of rocks, trees, eagles, views, and animals, of the wild kind.

One morning, my son Josh and I were working near the front of the land, driving in survey stakes to outline the location of the driveway. A neighbor was driving along the dirt road and spotted us. He pulled his pick-up over and climbed the hill to say hello. He asked if we were building and I said no, not soon, but I needed driveway access to the glen.

Looking around, he commented that this might be too shady a spot. Perhaps to the north a few hundred feet into the open field where the sun would melt the snow in the winter might be better. He mentioned that one of our neighbors had heavy equipment and he might be willing to put in the driveway. Great!

He then asked if I would be interested in having a phone line brought in. I laughed! Bring a phone line in without a house, with only a derelict trailer sitting on the side of the hill? Then he explained the reason for the question.

He mentioned the phone line which came into our high valley stopped several miles back down the road. His house was a few miles further along the mountain road. In order to have the phone company come in, dig the trench, and run the phone line to his house, he needed to find several people along this stretch of dirt road who would call the phone company and request service. He had four people so far who had done this. He just needed a couple more. If I would call and request a phone line, he would almost reach his goal to be qualified to receive phone service. My line would be brought up to a post near the old trailer. The continual generosity of my neighbors amazed me. I told him I would make the call. Then I pictured the pack rat climbing the post and answering the phone.

I asked him how he managed without phone service. He said he had arranged with the person at the end of the phone line, several miles back down the road, to have the phone company install a new phone line for him on the side of that person's barn. He then screwed a large mailbox onto the outside of the barn next to the line, placed a phone inside along with an answering machine powered by an outlet inside the barn, closed the mailbox and put a lock on it. Then once or twice a day he would drive there to get his messages and place phone calls. In every kind of weather! It was simple and ingenious.

Simple answers to big problems, that's a good principle to keep in mind when you're homesteading.

I visited my neighbor who owned the bulldozer. He and his wife had designed and built their log cabin: beautiful work, full basement, solar system, ample kitchen on the main floor, dining, living room, full bath, bedroom, loft. It was cozy in the worst winters with an outstanding view of the mountains from their windows and deck.

I described what I wanted regarding the driveway, and he agreed to put it in. He drove a semi for a major cross-country company and, after two weeks on the road, he came home stiff and achy. When he heard that I was a certified massage therapist, he said he would put in the driveway in exchange for massage therapy. When he got home from a trip, his wife would call and set up an appointment for me to come over. I would put my table in the back of my vehicle, drive to their house, and set up the table in the living room. (In addition to Swedish massage, I was trained in neuromuscular therapy, European hydrotherapy, deep tissue therapy, reflexology, and prenatal and postnatal massage.)

His wife trained horses and gave me my first riding lesson. It was a seven-mile trip through the hills with a group of neighbors. I felt that trip for a few days afterwards. Whoa!

That began a wonderful relationship with the neighbors as she told them about the massages I gave her husband and I picked up some clients there in the valley. We would get together for dinners and special occasions. Soon I had my driveway up into the glen, the trailer moved into its new spot, and a nice circle drive in front of the trailer.

Believe it or not, the phone did go in. When I finally ordered my service, because the trailer was a "temporary situation," the technician ran a line from the "pack rat" post at the old site to the present location of the trailer. I now had real phone service inside, with phones in the living room and the bedroom. I had moved up from the seventeenth century into the twentieth century, communication-wise, in one day. Now this was real living!

CHAPTER 10

The Storm

I saw the storm coming. It was a good twenty miles away, blocking out the sun in the west. Just the size of it should have warned me. I carried a couple of arm loads of firewood into the trailer and went back out to cover some things with tarps. I rolled up the windows of my truck. The storm was now fifteen miles away. I made a tour of the yard to make sure everything was tied down. This was summer, so there was no danger of snow but wind, rain, and hail were a constant danger. The weather and extremes of temperature at this altitude kept me on constant guard.

As the storm topped the mountains northwest of my valley, everything got dark. I could see the veil of rain sweeping across the valley but the wind and cold preceded it. Lightning flashed! Not just the occasional boom, but strike after strike marching right to my door! I ran inside and rolled the jalousie windows shut. I prayed for my huge ponderosas to be spared.

Kaboom! Kaboom! I grabbed my flashlight. Kaboom! I prayed my trailer would be spared. Kaboom! I didn't have lightning rods. The rains came fast and darkness engulfed the hillsides. Then with a noise louder than the rain and lightning, like a freight train rolling through the yard, came the hail thundering on my tin roof—what was left of it! I grabbed my Bible in one hand and held it to my chest, kneeling on the floor of the hall in the middle of the trailer, my flashlight the only light. The noise was so deafening I screamed out my prayers for mercy. I asked God to station His angels around the glen to diffuse the lightning strikes, to protect my roof, to protect me! No one else could have heard my prayers.

I don't know how long I huddled on the floor, but after a while I was aware of a strange, exhausted silence. The trailer creaked. I moved. Stretching my legs, I got up and looked toward the living room. Everything was still in place. Looking out the window I saw the ground covered in dense white, the weeds beaten down, most of the leaves of the aspens blasted into forlorn bits mixed with the hail. The landscape had been skinned alive!

Opening the front door, the cold air hit me, and the silence. The birds had sensed the ferocity of the storm and had fled to deep shelter. The chilled atmosphere dripped with eerie, shocked silence. In the distance, beyond the hills, I heard the dying grumblings of this unmerciful tempest.

Suddenly the western sun shot its healing photons under the receding gray vapor. As quickly as it had come, the hail began to melt. The leaves would compost into the soil. In a little while, the birds gave exploratory chirps and began to sing again. The tall spikes of meadow grass sprang up, shedding their icy weight. Soon the wild sage would bloom and fledglings would be nudged from their nests. And I could take a deep breath. Whew! Did I really want to live here in this wild mountain country? Oh, yes! And as I explored my land later, I saw that God had indeed spared my ponderosas. In the worst of the storm, He had heard my prayers.

A memory of a tale told by Dad came to mind. One afternoon, when we were young, he had been working down in our cellar. The rain was coming down; the darkness increased outside. The potbellied stove warmed the low-ceilinged room as he stood at the workbench, concentrating on a project. He heard a hiss and saw a bright light to his left. The pipes were all exposed in the cellar and there, sliding slowly down the pipe coming into the house from outside, was a sizzling fireball about the size of a basketball! He watched it without moving. He had heard the term "Great balls of fire!" and now he knew they were real. He stood very still, the hair on the back of his neck standing straight out. When it reached a bend in the pipe it turned and slowly moved horizontally along it.

For several minutes it crept along the pipe. He prayed that Mom would not open the cellar door and start to come down. This would be the very time she would be coming to get one or more of her canning jars of vegetables to fix for dinner.

Holding his breath, his eyes never left the ball of fire and then suddenly with a loud "pop" it disappeared. He stood there a minute, looking at the pipe and the concrete wall to make sure there was nothing burned or charred. He moved closer to inspect the stairs because the pipe went right behind them. All was safe but there was a strange smell in the air, if balls of fire or electricity can have a smell. He walked around the cellar to check everything out. Then he took a big breath and climbed the stairs with quite a tale to tell all of us.

After this storm, I learned to keep an eye on the sky. I hung Dad's weather station on the living room wall: barometer, thermometer, and hygrometer. Now I checked this several times a day. With no power, radios won't work, so I could not get a weather report. In the mornings my eyes scanned the skies, especially toward the west. I learned to read the clouds and feel the humidity or lack thereof. How fast was the air moving? Were there upslope conditions? Were the birds happy, singing, and busy, or silent? Were the deer around, the cattle grazing peacefully? All right. At least for a few hours I could split some wood and get my walk in.

My sense of hearing improved dramatically without the interference of artificial sound. I could hear dogs bark over on another mountain. Voices traveled. Chain saws echoed. I could hear the occasional vehicle go by on the dirt road a quarter of a mile away. Decades ago, early in the morning the train whistle could still be heard fifteen miles away.

With no artificial noise, my ears became one with my mountain. A browsing bear cub would be identified before it saw me and scampered up the hill. I wanted the bear to know I was there. The birds were my best warning system. When their normal songs and calls turned to alarm I knew they'd spotted me or there was something else in the area.

My peripheral vision also sharpened. I don't know if it was the higher altitude, the clean air, the pure well water, the daily exercise of walking around on the side of the mountain, or no fast food, but my vision improved noticeably. I didn't need to wear my glasses. I could clearly see the line of trees on the next mountain and count the trees on the skyline. I used to have Air Force vision growing up. Now it seemed to be coming back.

I was healthier living on my mountain than I had been for many years at the lower altitudes. My weight went down, my waist narrowed, my muscles grew stronger, and I even got a few whistles. I worked three days a week at a day spa as a massage therapist, so I kept in good shape. My meals were simple and always eaten with thanksgiving and humility—fresh vegetables sliced and eaten raw or lightly steamed; oatmeal cooked with chopped apples and raisins and sprinkled with cinnamon and honey; sardines on rye crackers; baked beans, cold, with sliced tomatoes and a piece of cheese or avocado; various sandwiches. Not a lot of foods that needed refrigeration. I was grateful for simple things. A glass of water to quench my thirst. A sunny window in which to sit. A book to read. My Bible.

I remember on several occasions I would become aware of a permeating dampness at night. I would look out the window and see nothing but fog. It was cold. I opened the door and stepped out onto the deck. Turning on my flashlight the beam stretched into the fog. I felt tiny spritzes on my face and arms—it was ice! The fog had frozen and was settling on my arms and face in the most minute ice crystals. It felt good. Yes, even though it was summer, we still got freezing temperatures at night.

Living outside as much as inside enabled me to monitor weather patterns. After the hail storm, I called to price lightning rods or cables. The cheapest lightning rod system was eleven hundred dollars, more than two months Social Security. I had to do without. But my trust in God became strong and stronger with each passing event. I could trust Him and I knew He heard my prayers.

CHAPTER 11

Reading by Oil Lamps

Back inside the trailer on the mountain, my oil lamps had to be ready to light. I had to know where the matches were in the dark. It was easier to carry a cigarette lighter in my pocket. I could not depend on walking into the house at night and being able to simply turn on the lamps. Preparation for that had to begin in the morning right after the breakfast dishes were done.

In Exodus, I read that Aaron the priest would light the altar of incense in the morning so the sweet aroma of prayers could rise to God. While the aroma of incense was rising, he cleaned the lamps of the menorah, getting it ready to light. It pleased me to think about the priests setting the example for the rest of us.

Carrying all the lamps to the kitchen counter, I removed each chimney and washed them in hot, soapy water to remove the soot, then rinsed and dried them with a paper towel. Then I filled the bowl of each lamp with oil, replaced the clean chimney, and carried each lamp back to its spot: one at each end of the sofa, one on the kitchen counter, one in the bathroom, and one in the bedroom.

It was important to keep a good supply of lamp oil in the kitchen cabinet. I wasn't going to run out at night, driving down a curvy dirt mountain road, dodging deer for forty miles, for lamp oil. And after dark, about eight o'clock, most of the neighbors were asleep. So preparation for night began in the morning.

Scripture tells of ten virgins who were waiting for the arrival of the King (Matt. 25: 1–13). They all had oil in their lamps but five of them carried extra oil. Five unhappy young virgins had to learn a devastating lesson for not having extra oil on hand. They did not prepare for the night during the day. They thought they could borrow oil from the other virgins. The oil represents the Holy Spirit and the Word of God. They hadn't studied enough of the Word to know they needed the oil of the Holy Spirit and to store up the Word of God in their hearts that they might not sin against Him.

Because I did so much reading and writing by oil lamps, I had to devise a way to raise the wattage of each lamp, as I mentioned before. I tore off a twenty-inch piece of aluminum foil. In the middle of one long edge, I crimped over an inch or two of foil so it could hang on the top of the glass chimney. I spread out the sides to form "wings" to reflect the light onto my work. It turned one flame into the brightness of three or four.

All my writing was done by hand. With no power, computers were useless. I loved the quiet time in the evenings to put down my thoughts. There in the silence, the events of the day came to life on the paper.

I found I could save money by not buying lamp oil in grocery or big outlet stores. While getting gas one day, I noticed a gas pump that dispensed kerosene. Purchasing a metal gas can, I could fill up with kerosene on my way home from shopping. One thing to keep in mind when using oil lamps is good ventilation. I always had that as my jalousie windows were never tight. There was always a slight draft coming and going through those windows. One other caution: be careful if you have cats. One of my neighbors lit an oil lamp during a storm and her cat's tail caught on fire when his tail got too close to the chimney. Yeoooww! Be even more careful with candles.

At night, when all my reading and writing were done, all the lamps would be turned off but one. This one was at the end of the hall. I swiveled its foil shade around to shine down the hall and turned the flame low. This was my night light. It prevented many a stubbed toe. It also made my home feel not quite so lonely.

CHAPTER 12

Fire Control

Sometimes storms come up in the afternoon with dark clouds that require the lighting of one or two lamps. The mountains are famous for afternoon storms. Lightning has started fires in my high valley. One of our neighbors has an old fire truck with a water tank, which he keeps filled for just such emergencies.

One afternoon, as I was getting my supper, a storm came through, lightning flashed, and a fire started deep down in the roots of a tree on the other side of the mountain. It didn't become visible until the next day. The fire spread to a field and the neighbors poured into the area with trucks, backhoes, and bulldozers to create a firebreak. Some directed traffic so the tank truck could get through. Others brought water for the men to drink. Call the fire company? Of course they did. However, they were twenty-plus dirt-road miles away. Cabins struck by lightning in the area had burned to the ground waiting for fire trucks to arrive. The people in the valley knew they had to act fast. The neighbors were the first responders. They were a team. They were responsible. They were prepared. Within seconds of the call, they were out the door and moving their vehicles toward the fire to help their neighbors.

I heard the commotion along the road that evening, and called a neighbor to find out what was going on. A lot of traffic was going in one direction including heavy equipment. "Oh, yes, there's a big fire on the other side of the mountain. All the guys are headed over to help put it out." I didn't smell any smoke. The wind must have been blowing toward the south away from me. I waited a while and prayed for the men and the safety of the people and the homes. The next morning the good report went out that they had been successful in putting out the fire.

I remember decades ago visiting a family who lived in Topanga Canyon in California. The husband had installed several sprinklers on his roof as part of his fire protection. He had the sprinklers connected to a pump that would draw water from his swimming pool and spray the roof and yard in case of fire. Some years later a fire did come through that canyon and he put his system into operation. His was the only house in the canyon that survived the fire.

When I am finally ready to build on my property, I will also install such a system on my house. I may not have a swimming pool but I can have a large cistern installed higher up on the hill which will allow gravity to feed water to those sprinklers in time of emergency. I will also keep my yard clear of underbrush and keep woodpiles away from the house.

It's a good idea to not build a house with a shake roof. It can catch on fire and hasten the destruction of the house. Asphalt shingles melt but a corrugated steel roof or Spanish tile is better. Remember the wildfires in Colorado? One man's house didn't burn because it was built entirely of concrete. Even the "wood" trim around the windows was of concrete, painted in accent colors to coordinate with the rest of the house; upon close examination you could not tell it was concrete. Expensive but apparently well worth it.

With no cell phone towers in our valley, it's necessary to have land line phones. A fire in the area is one time it's essential to have good communication between homes. Reverse 911 helps, too. Having a good plan of action makes all the difference. Handy fire extinguishers in home and vehicle can stop small problems. A tractor can plow a fire break around a home. Common sense helps too. Having coded street numbers will enable firemen to find you quickly. Those who dial 911 need to be ready to answer questions and give directions. They can't just say, "My house is on fire!" and hang up. The fire department needs a name and address.

Firefighters pride themselves in having five-minute response times. Obviously this is not possible in remote areas. Each family should have their own plan in any emergency. It is wise for every member of the family to have a backpack, suitcase, or duffle bag—packed with an extra set of clothes, snacks, flashlight, extra batteries, a bottle of water, warm jacket or raincoat, and even a few family pictures—set aside in their closet, ready to grab and go in any emergency.

If people have animals, they need to let them loose. Remember the old movies? The horses and cows were taken out of the barn. At a time like this, their safety is in the fields. Pets can be piled into vehicles. People need to stay cool-headed and follow the plan, trusting the precautions they have taken to protect their place. They should do what they can, but be ready to leave if necessary. They need to trust what the firefighters say. They know their business and how to protect people. They will direct people to a safe place. Remember, people are more important than their house. Go in faith.

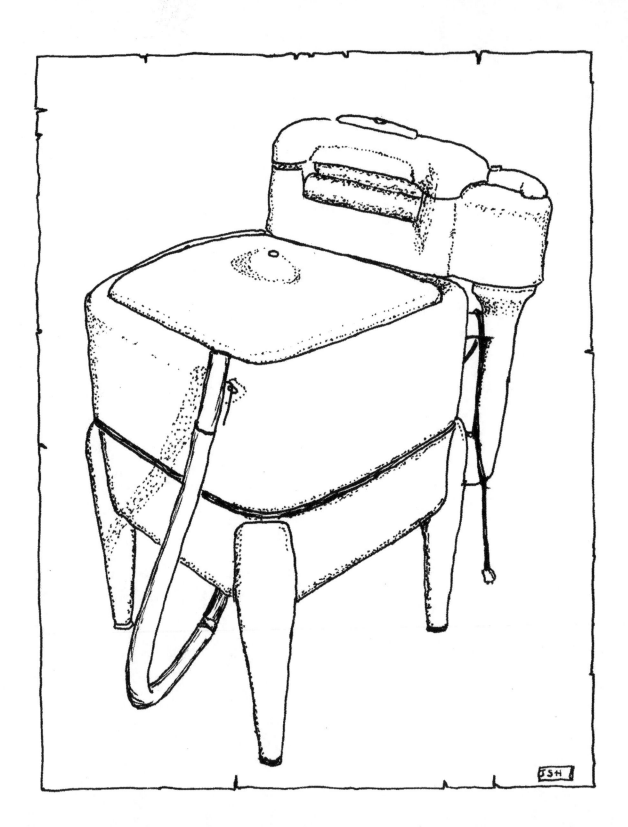

CHAPTER 13

Waterworks

Do we really appreciate running water? We turn on the faucet and let the water run while we brush our teeth. We wash our hands a dozen times a day. We plop the clothes into the washing machine, push a button, and walk away. The water and the machine do the rest. The timer turns on the sprinklers to water the yard. Not so, on my mountain. People here don't have lawns.

All my neighbors have wells. There are no water lines. A prospective homebuilder contacts the drilling company. A technician drives up to check out the land and the location of the house.

It is mandatory to have a well first before you build and the well must produce at least three to five gallons per minute for the well to be declared good. The technician dowses for the best spot for water on the land. He sets up his rig and starts drilling.

He will usually find surface water first, which is run-off water. This would give the landowner a shallow well and would be subject to the seasons. He needs to find an aquifer, which is a large underground pool or lake. Deep water. Pure water. The underground stream can dry up in a drought. The aquifer has been there for thousands of years. The driller needs to go down until he finds it.

How did the pioneers find water? How did Abraham, Isaac, and Jacob find water? As they moved they had to find another well and another. The people around them claimed the water as theirs. They moved again. They prayed. The Lord was faithful. They found water.

Jacob's well is still there. Jesus drank from it when He spoke to the Samaritan woman and offered her Living Water. The Samaritan woman took it. She had been looking for spiritual water as she approached the physical well. She found Jesus, the Living Water, the Water of Life.

Next to air, water is our most precious commodity. This is evident in other countries where drought conditions have been going on for decades. We send money to finance the drilling of wells so communities can have pure, clean water instead of drinking out of muddy puddles or alligator-infested rivers. These people don't know the difference. I played in mud puddles when I was a girl but I never thought of drinking that water. Why? Because I knew even at that early age it was dirty. Wasn't that a worm drowning in there? Besides, I knew there was fresh pure water just inside the house. I knew the difference.

In my mountain home, I ran my household on thirty-two gallons of water a week. That's correct; I did everything on thirty-two gallons each week. It's amazing how far water can be stretched when it is scarce. My old trailer had no functioning pipes. They had rusted out over the years the trailer had been abandoned on the mountain. The only running water I had was when I ran over to another mountain in my vehicle with eight two-gallon plastic jugs to fill them up at one of my neighbor's wells. Twice a week I made the trip to different neighbors.

I recycled water as much as possible. I heated it in my twelve-quart soup kettle on the woodstove for washing dishes, rinsed them from a two–and-a-half gallon plastic jug with a spigot, on a shelf behind the sink, letting that water run into the dishpan so none was wasted. If the dishwater cooled too much, I simply dipped a saucepan into the dishpan filling it with soapy water and put it on the woodstove to reheat, then poured the hot dish water back into the dishpan. When the dishes were done, I used that same water to wipe off the counter and wash the kitchen floor. If there was more left over, I used it to clean the bathroom.

Since most of the pipes were rusted or missing, I improvised my own drainage system. I did not want to go under the trailer, however, it could not be avoided. Since the ground was sloped, the back end of the trailer was touching the ground and the front was about five feet off the ground. It was propped up with concrete blocks.

Crawling under the trailer, I located the pipe coming down from the kitchen sink. Using lots of duct tape, I attached a large mechanic's plastic funnel with a long curved spout, open end up, to the bottom of the sink pipe. I stuck the small end into another pipe which went into a four-inch by ten-foot white plastic pipe going away from the trailer. I had very nice healthy vegetation at the end of that pipe.

I'm an old scout, so I know how to brush my teeth with one cup of water and how to take a sponge bath. There was no such thing as a shower before one ingenious, sweaty person grabbed a bucket, stabbed the bottom full of holes with an ice pick, ran to a stream, filled it up with water, hung it from a branch, and took the first shower. Ahhhh.

Today's camping version of that is called a "sun shower," which is a plastic bag holding about two or three gallons of water, usually black on one side to absorb the sun's heat. With a tube and a small shower head attached, it was set in the sun for an hour or so, and then hung from a tree. I could take a full shower, shampoo, and rinse my hair in two-and-a-half gallons of water. I hung mine in the bathtub from the shower head. For daily sponge bathing, I put a half gallon of hot water in a large stainless steel bowl. It was similar to the way people used to bathe two hundred fifty to three hundred years ago or more, before running water. Each room had a pitcher and bowl on the wash stand but their water was cold. They bathed and shaved with whatever the pitcher held.

I usually waited until mid-afternoon to shower, when the trailer had a chance to warm up in the sun so I wouldn't get chilled. I dried my hair outside in the sun just as I remembered doing as a girl when my hair was so long I could sit on it.

A brief description of my washday follows:

Every week, I washed and rinsed two loads of clothes by hand in about seven or eight gallons of water. I heated the water in my twelve-quart soup kettle on the woodstove. I poured some of the water into a large plastic bowl or dishpan in the double sink. I poured more water into another bowl or dishpan in the other sink for rinsing. I put the kettle back onto the woodstove and added more water to heat for the next load. Into the first dishpan I put clothing detergent, a tad bit of bleach, and the light clothes. I let them soak, swishing them around for a few minutes. I didn't have a scrub board, but scrubbed each article of clothing by hand. Squeezing out all the soapy water, I put each piece in the rinse water. After I squeezed all the rinse water out of the light clothes, I added the rinse water to the first dishpan and added more detergent. In went the dark clothes to soak. You see that I used the rinse water twice. I repeated the process with that load.

Before I rinsed the dark clothes, I rinsed the light clothes again in the fresh hot water. This gave them two good rinses. I squeezed the water out of the light clothes before I put them into the laundry basket. While the dark clothes soaked, I carried the first load out to the clothesline strung between three trees and pinned them up. (Fortunately, they still make clothespins.) I used a forked pole to prop up the heavy line in the middle. The breezes coming across the valley were just enough to dry them in about an hour or so.

I went back in and scrubbed and rinsed the second load with a final clean water rinse and hung them up. The heavier blue jeans and towels would take longer to dry. I usually left clothes on the line until mid to late afternoon to absorb the warmth of the sun. Of course, I had to keep an eye on the weather to prevent a rain storm from undoing my work. The clothes smelled so good, it was worth the effort. That was my wash day.

As an additional note, since I had no power and could not use an iron, I took my nice dress clothes to the cleaners so they were always neat.

On rainy days I hung my clothes on a line in front of the woodstove. They dried quickly and provided needed humidity in the trailer.

A dry stream bed runs diagonally across the land. There had been water in the stream at some time in the past but something had caused the water to go underground. Perhaps a slight shift in the earth, or a rock blocking the flow had forced the water down into some porous gravel. I have asked the Lord to loosen whatever is blocking the flow of water from above and let the stream flow as before.

I explored more of the property. I climbed up the steep slope through the tall ponderosas and noticed many young aspen trees, which is a sign of plentiful water. Near the top of the next shoulder I found new young trees growing, indicating more good water across that plateau. There was no shortage of water on my property! However it made sense to drill a well near the proposed location of the house. Now I knew why I had so many aspen trees on my place. I made a quick estimate of about fifteen hundred to two thousand aspens. They were thriving.

Contacting a well driller, I found the cost of drilling a well ran about ten to twelve thousand dollars, depending upon the depth. He told me how to apply for a well-drilling permit. The cost just for the permit was four hundred and eighty dollars! That was close to one months' Social Security. It would have to wait.

When I went into town, I would buy several large two-and-a-half gallon plastic containers of water along with my groceries. These were handy because they have spouts and could be refilled with a small funnel when the spout was pulled out. I was careful to punch just a tiny hole in the top with a pin to let in air, which prevented water from spilling when it was carried. This allowed the jugs to be refilled many times.

Several years after my pilgrimage on the mountain, I was able to have my well drilled. The driller went down 285 feet and found sweet fresh water from an aquifer with a flow of eight-and-a-half gallons a minute. That's more than enough water to qualify for a house.

Water is wonderful! It quenches your thirst, cleans your clothes, bathes your body, waters your garden, freshens the air, forms clouds in the sky, washes your car, lets you swim in lakes and rivers, crashes in waves at the sea shore. Next to air, it is our most important, precious commodity. Cherish it.

CHAPTER 14

Staying Healthy

In addition to working as a massage therapist, I kept in shape by walking along the dirt road with two pound hand weights. I didn't have the sophisticated hand weights that are available now. I race walked for a couple miles north then back south to my driveway. The altitude was approximately nine thousand feet. I carried water and stopped to rest as needed.

Moving around on my property was a constant form of exercise. Carrying in firewood, splitting wood, raking the area in front of the trailer to keep it neat, used all my muscles. A hike up to the top of the land from the trailer, which was about two hundred feet higher, always left me breathless. I not only carried water but took my hiking stick along. I hammered a nail into the top of the stick and snipped off the head as an additional protection against predators. It may not have given me much protection but it made me feel safer.

Once at the top, I sat down on the highest rock and looked out over the valley. I would drink some water and munch on a cookie or chips and let my eyes wander over the far mountains and valleys. As the sun reached toward its zenith, shadows decreased. I would bring out a notebook and write my thoughts and munch some more on the snack. Some form of salt became important to me as I was outside so much of the time and sweated off my moisture. In the cooler weather I learned to keep a cap on my head because much of the body heat is lost quickly through the head. I usually climbed to the top in the mornings as the afternoons could bring storms and I wanted to avoid lightning. I gave myself different assignments each day. One day I would climb up the Bear trail. The next I would walk up the dry brook. Another day I would cut through the ponderosas and around the ridge of moss rock to a higher outcropping on the south. Then there is a copse of scrub oak to the west that the deer love and I go there to watch the sunset.

How can so much peace become available simply by the elimination of the manmade sounds of civilization? We open our ears to the evensong of the variety of bird calls—the bunting, the thrush, the wren, the hummer after the last few sips at the feeder, the wild swish of the great white owl through the glen beginning his search for dinner, and the call of the night hawk as he skims overhead.

I remember years ago, when we camped on the mountain as a family, our oldest son Mike would wander over to the knoll covered with scrub oak, sit on a fallen log with his guitar, and begin singing while he played. In a few minutes, out of the corner of our eyes, we noticed some cows climbing the hill. More came into view and stood watching and listening to him play. They formed an audience, attentive and appreciative, edging closer into a group. We had to collar our dog, which happened to be a border collie. This was a perfect picture of my idea of a young David, sitting out on a hillside in the evenings, playing and singing to his sheep, calming their fears about any wild beasts prowling in the area. This is a favorite memory of mine when I wander around on the land and am tempted to feel lonely or afraid. Besides, God's angels are encamped around us as we sip our evening tea.

The water I drank was exclusively well water. I made tea and hot chocolate with it and reconstituted orange juice. The water had no chlorine, fluoride, or any chemicals as city water would. It had a sweet, clean taste. I drank it straight as it came from the well. Now today, I would add a few drops of colloidal silver to my glass or a teaspoon full to the pitcher. (See chapter 22 for more about colloidal silver.) When doing my dishes I always added a few drops of bleach to the dishwater to aid in killing germs. I also used bleach on my cutting boards. This is especially wise when you have animals or live around livestock. Today I would put colloidal silver in my pet's water dish and if I have chickens and goats sometime, I will plan to put colloidal silver in their drinking water. This could keep them healthy and protect them from whatever is going around. (This hint would be a wise consideration for anyone who has large poultry ranches.) Cleanliness and sanitation are important since cattle and deer are in my yard almost daily, not to mention the occasional bear and most likely the cougar, coyotes, and wolves that tour my land at night; yes, even now.

In the mornings, spending time in the sun is actually a healthy way to get vitamin D. The sun's rays are absorbed through the oils in our skin and make vitamin D. Because I have had some skin cancer, I found that a good way for me to get the vitamin D I needed was to place about a quarter cup of olive oil in a saucer, place it out in the yard where it can absorb bright sunlight for an hour or so, bring it in and rub it into my skin. This was a handy idea when I ran out of my supplements. Nutritionist Adele Davis recommended this simple solution years ago in her books *Let's Get Well*, *Let's Eat Right to Keep Fit*, and *Let's Have Healthy Children*. The sun forms vitamin D in the oil. This was the most natural way to get the vitamin D I needed without increasing the danger of skin cancer. This could even be done all winter long when more time is spent indoors. Besides, our skin loves olive oil with or without vitamin D.

As a massage therapist, I am asked questions about how to keep skin soft, especially in a dry climate. What I recommend to my clients is to rub on olive oil right after a shower and then immediately put some hand or body lotion on top of the oil. It's a rich combination and, after a few hours or overnight, the skin is so soft. A lotion with Shea butter also works well. But watch your step. Don't put any oil on the bottoms of your feet unless you put on socks or slippers.

As a reflexologist, I learned the importance of a good foot massage with deep tissue therapy and to give myself a great pedicure. Soaking the feet in water is scriptural, as Jesus washed the feet of the disciples. Soaking feet in a basin of warm water with Epsom salts and essential oils softens the skin and the nails, which makes trimming the nails easier. A pumice stone removes tough callous. After I dried my feet, I then sprayed them with my travel bottle of colloidal silver water. This acts as a moisturizer to the skin and also kills germs and helps to lessen problems like athlete's foot or any areas of fungus on the nails.

I learned to make natural ointments with olive oil and beeswax, adding some fresh herbs according to the need. Essential oils work well also. Dried herbs can be found at health food stores for very reasonable prices.

The process was quite simple; I collected the herbs I needed for the ointment: mint or camphor leaves from a tree we had when we lived in the South, sassafras tree leaves we had living in the Northeast, chamomile flowers. I tried one or two for each ointment. I borrowed an herb book from the library to see specifically how each herb was used traditionally in the past. I have also added several good herb books to my library.

In a saucer, the leaves or root were crushed with the back of a spoon. I poured about two tablespoons of olive oil into a small saucepan, then added the wax from the honeycomb after the honey had been eaten or drained, about two ounces. Then the crushed herbs were added to the oil mixture and heated on low. I was careful not to boil, but to only heat it until the wax melts into the oil, stirring to distribute the herbs. After removing the pan from the heat, I allowed it to cool slowly for a few minutes. The longer the herbs stay in the ointment, the more potent the ointment. This allows the essence of the herbs to permeate the mixture well. Then, before it cooled completely, I poured it into clean jars. Old make-up jars work well.

I remember as a young girl finding ginseng in our woods back home. At the time I didn't know what it was. By studying herb books since then, I have been able to identify it. My sister and I used to pull off honeysuckle flowers and suck out the sweet nectar. There was just a drop per flower but it was so delicious. Take a walk around your area and see what fresh herbs you can identify.

Mom would send me outside with scissors to cut some fresh mint to put in homemade iced tea. She listened to Dr. Carlton Fredericks on the radio and was way before her time feeding us healthy foods and herbs. She would give my sister and me cod liver oil in the mornings along with our breakfast before we went to school. She also squeezed fresh orange juice for us. There's nothing like it.

Woods and fields are rich places to look for herbs and wild flowers. I have wild sage growing on my land. I also have small wild roses that produce rose hips in the fall. Pinion trees produce pine nuts, which are hard to harvest but worth the effort. They go well in salads or nut breads.

For the first two years I lived on my land, I did not have a working oven. I did all my cooking on a woodstove. I bought my bread for this reason, even though I know how to bake my own fresh bread. I purchased a second-hand gas stove and a gas-powered refrigerator—a big blessing in the third year. A neighbor helped me hook up a one–hundred-pound propane tank outside the trailer. He ran a line into the kitchen and hooked it up to the refrigerator and gas stove. Now I could heat my water on the stove right in my kitchen. The propane would last about a month and then I would unhook it, tip it into the back of my pickup truck, brace it with two concrete blocks, and drive it into town to have it refilled. When I got home I tipped it out of the truck and reattached it.

Living in remote areas, one needs to plan for possible emergencies. I had to have a plan in the event that I might fall and injure myself. It really pays to have an automatic vehicle. With most injuries it would be possible to drive with one good hand or foot either to a neighbor's place or even into town. A well- stocked first aid kit is a must. Band-Aids can handle most small injuries but iodine, alcohol, strips of gauze and some Ace bandages are handy for abrasions and sprained ankles. The new Ace bandages now stretch and stick in place without the need of clips. Ice is good on a fresh injury to keep down the swelling and reduce pain but it is a luxury in the mountains unless you have electricity to run a refrigerator with a freezer. My newly acquired Servel gas refrigerator had a small freezer and I was able to make ice cubes. In the winter, it would be possible to pack an injury with snow.

Once I slipped on the front steps early in the morning when there was a thin layer of black ice on the damp wood. (This is proof that the temperatures do get below freezing at night in the mountains in the summer.) I caught my thumb on a board and turned my nail back. Cleaning the area with alcohol, I wrapped my entire thumb with gauze and masking tape, creating an effective splint that enabled me to continue working. Duct tape would also work.

Whenever I went hiking, I made a practice of carrying a hunting knife in a sheath on my belt and a canteen of cold water. A scarf around my neck could make a quick bandage. Even salt from chips in a zipper bag could disinfect a cut. A hundred years ago or more, honey was used to treat burns. It was thought to hasten healing, drawing out moisture with its hygroscopic action, disinfecting and sealing the wound.

Another thing I had to think about was vitamins and minerals in a primitive situation. I couldn't afford to buy much in the way of supplements. I had previously been able to recover from a bronchial cold with the help of a simple solution of colloidal silver. I had access to a colloidal silver generator with which I made a solution of colloidal silver in about fifteen minutes. The generator was made up of three nine volt batteries, wired in-series, connected by alligator clips to two six-inch strands of 99.99 percent pure silver wire, one positive and one negative. The wires were immersed into a quart size jar of water, without touching, and timed for ten to fifteen minutes. I could see bubbles coming up from one wire and "mist" coming up from the other wire. The twenty-seven volts from the batteries through electrostatic action removed and suspended .5 micron sized bits of

99.99 percent pure silver throughout the water. Only plastic spoons could touch the water because any metal would short circuit the electrostatic charge and the silver would then precipitate to the bottom of the jar.

I dipped a plastic serving spoon into the jar and placed the fresh colloidal silver water into orange juice, stirring and drinking it with my breakfast. I could have just added it to water but it has a slightly metallic taste. Silver is a natural mineral that our bodies need in minute amounts. Doing this each day was just enough over the next five days to help me recover from my bronchial cold. By using three nine-volt batteries I could make this anywhere and not need electricity. Now more advanced generators are available which make a higher grade of colloidal silver and new research has discovered many more ways it can boost the immune system helping us to fight flu and virus infections. One source is listed in the back of this book.

You may wonder how anyone ever found out about silver and health. You've heard the expression, "born with a silver spoon in his mouth." Back when the wealthy ate on silver plates or with silverware that was 100 percent silver, they automatically got silver in their diets every day.

In pioneer days, Grandma would drop a silver dollar into the milk jug to keep the milk fresh longer. She may not have known exactly why it worked but she knew it did. Silver kills germs and bacteria.

Continually needing to purchase vitamins and minerals in my primitive situation would have been expensive. I solved that problem by sprouting seeds. Sprouted wheat and lentils are very nutritious. They can be added to salads for a hefty boost in nutrition. Elsewhere in this book, in the chapter on woodstove cooking, I have a recipe for sprouted lentil salad. The last chapter in the book, "Saved by Seeds," tells how to sprout seeds and how they can be used.

It's great to know I could leave my house for the day with a good nourishing meal under my belt. I grabbed the water canteen, a piece of fruit and other snacks, a tiny first-aid kit, a pocket knife and maybe a book in my day pack. A small notebook let me write down my thoughts. Wearing a hat with a wide brim kept the sun off my face and neck. It was also great if the weather changed and I ran into rain. I've learned to wear layers and a windbreaker with a sweatshirt underneath, providing extra insulation on a cold, windy day. Following simple common sense rules makes me feel confident when I know I am taking good care of myself.

Common sense also kept me inside on rainy days. I read books from my impromptu library. I started my library by going to a second-hand store where people brought their used books. I could buy a paper grocery sack full of books of my choice for two dollars, even an entire encyclopedia. I reacquainted myself with many of the old classics: *Twenty Thousand Leagues Under the Sea, Swiss Family Robinson* (might I be related to this family?) and others. This is what rainy days are for, aren't they? A good book, some hot chocolate or cup of tea, and the warmth of a woodstove. Mmmm.

CHAPTER 15

April Snows Bring ... More April Snows

I remember stepping outside the door one evening to look at the stars. As I stood on the old wooden deck, I felt cold pinpoints hitting my face. I was surrounded with a slowly moving effervescent cloud. I looked at my arms and they were covered with minute ice crystals. The cloud was freezing and precipitating miniature snow specks onto my sleeves. I looked up at the moon through the heavy cloud and the glen caught the glow and turned itself into a mystical, moving, floating ice shower on my face, my hair, the leaves of the aspens, the grass. I breathed in the cool beauty as the cloud drifted down the hill. A few stars showed themselves as the cloud thinned out here and there. I blew into it and watched my breath freeze and be carried off as part of the cloud. What fun! Angels could have been dancing overhead and felt right at home.

I didn't want to go inside. I didn't want to leave this place, but it was September and I knew the time was coming soon. In another month the leaves would start to turn and fall, the nights would get colder and longer, the winds would come and then the snow. This derelict trailer was no place to be in deep snow for any length of time, no place to even think of spending a winter, let alone the mountains of firewood I would need.

I thought about the previous April. The weather doesn't play fair up at nine thousand feet. It was snowing when I went to bed that night in the middle of April. In the morning the trailer was shivering cold. I loaded the woodstove up with more logs. Then I looked out the window and grabbed the yardstick. Whoa! I put on a warm coat, scarf and hat. Boots, yes! Fortunately the door opened in and not out as with some trailers.

I stuck the yardstick into the snow on the porch. Twenty-eight inches and still coming down. I used the broom in an attempt to sweep the snow off the deck. I went back inside to find the ash shovel to the woodstove. That worked better. I sprinkled some ash from the ash bucket onto the deck. That helped to keep me from slipping. I did more shoveling and put ash onto the steps. Using a broom to clear the drive around my truck got me almost nowhere. Why did I think I might not need a snow shovel in the mountains in April?

With the depth of the snow I realized I would not be able to make my massage appointments in town. I had no idea whether the dirt roads had been plowed. I was thirty-five hundred feet higher than the river, and then needed to climb back up to another high mountain valley. Forty miles in fresh snow? No! Fortunately, I had a phone. I went inside to cancel the appointments. By that time there were thirty inches of snow and the skies were giving hints of clearing. I carried more logs into the trailer and let them warm up next to the stove. This was going to be one of those days for good books and hot chocolate. Yum.

Two weeks later, at the end of April, I woke up so cold! I couldn't understand why the bed was chilly. Besides flannel sheets, I had on four blankets topped with a lovely down comforter. The mattress felt cold. The air was frigid. I could see my breath! The freezing carpet fibers crunched when my feet hit the floor!

I set a mountain top record for getting dressed and headed for the living room. The woodstove was out, cold. The oil lamp which I leave on at night set very low was still burning. It was the warmest thing in the house. I held my hands over the top of the chimney to warm them. Then I glanced over at the weather station on the wall. It said twenty-four degrees! That was in the living room! What must it have been in the bedroom twenty feet down the hall? I didn't want to know. Just get this trailer warmed up!

I had to start from scratch building a new fire, rolling up newspapers, tying them in knots just like my dad used to do decades ago. I loaded them into the stove along with some tinder, small sticks, and lit it all with the cigarette lighter which I always carried in my pocket. While the fire was getting started, I continued to warm up my hands over the oil lamp chimney.

The soup kettle of water was as icy as the air, so I placed it over the hottest spot near the stovepipe. The coffee pot went right next to it. I lifted another pot from its hook on the wall for oatmeal. When that water was measured and heating I started beating up some eggs to scramble. I put two pieces of bread into some butter melting in the frying pan. When one side was toasted, I flipped them over and toasted the other side. Removing the toast, I put a spoonful of cream cheese in the middle of the eggs in the frying pan. As the eggs cooked, the cheese melted. When the water was hot, I poured some into my mug and added some instant milk powder, stirring it and adding in a package of hot chocolate mix. Mmm. I was beginning to warm up.

If this sounds like an enormous meal, it was just the kind of meal I needed to fortify my metabolism. I looked outside and discovered another huge snow storm. That's why my world was so frigid. This time I measured forty inches. I knew my energies would be needed to deal with this load of white. The branches of the pines and ponderosas groaned under this new load and I heard occasional cracking sounds as branches would falter and snap off, land on top of other lower branches and overload those and so on down the height of the tree. A few days later a walk up the mountainside revealed the damage. One ponderosa was totally stripped of branches, all of which lay scattered on the ground. On others, the lower branches were gone. My heart hurt for my trees.

After breakfast I cleaned off my deck but didn't bother making a path for my truck. I simply picked up the phone cancel my appointments again. Believe me, I could ill afford to give up three or four appointments with regular massage clients, but I didn't argue with forty inches of snow.

CHAPTER 16

Kittens

The two yellow tiger kittens came to me in this way. My neighbor three miles down the road had a barn in which she kept farm equipment, feed for her horses, tools, and a canoe. She was feeding her barn cats one morning when she heard tiny mewling sounds somewhere in the barn. Looking around she found nothing. Almost giving up she turned as she realized the sounds were coming from overhead. Her canoe was suspended from the barn rafters. Lowering the canoe, she found two yellow tiger kittens, one black kitten, one mottled kitten, and two calicos. They were less than a week old.

She showed her husband and he built a strong cage of redwood two-by-fours and wire mesh where he placed the kittens after they were weaned. They brought the cage into the house and set it on the kitchen floor. They were safe from the household dogs but allowed to get used to being around people. Several of us neighbors chose kittens and paid ten dollars to have them fixed. When they were ten weeks old, we took them, all together, to be spayed/neutered in town. After they healed, we each took our kitties home. I took two because I thought they would keep each other company and play together. This proved to be a good decision.

One evening, when the kittens were about three months old, it was quite dark outside and I had all my oil lamps lit. I became aware of noises in the lower kitchen cabinets. The kittens heard it too and had crept closer to investigate. What a wonderful opportunity, I thought, to teach them about catching mice! Their attention was absolutely focused on the two middle doors under the sink. I moved forward softly and reached down to pull the doors open wide. As I did so, there in the center sat an eight-inch-tall pack rat. He didn't move a whisker. He spotted the kittens at the same moment they spotted him. They smelled him but he never moved.

Suddenly it occurred to me that this was a large wild animal to them, fat and vicious, wily in the ways of the mountains. My kittens, just three months old, might have been torn to shreds. Making an instant decision, I slammed the doors shut and heard the pack rat knocking things over scurrying away. The kittens crept closer and I reopened the doors. They investigated the smell of the pack rat and entered the cabinet. They needed to know their enemy. When they were bigger they could fight to the death. For now they would eat and grow and prepare for that day. Just like me, reading and eating the Word, growing and preparing for the days I need to face the enemy in victory.

CHAPTER 17

Wild Dogs

Earlier, before I moved the trailer and had it relocated to its present location, I had spent the night. Waking up the next morning, looking out the windows, I could see nothing but white mist. An upslope condition had moved into the area during the night and the trees dripped with dew. I was hungry, so I decided some fog was not going to stop me from cooking breakfast. The fog was so thick I could not see twenty feet. I was literally in a cloud at nine thousand two hundred feet.

An old stone fireplace, very rough, had been formed in the rocks of a bank with two side rocks. I placed a grate on these two rocks and built my fire. I had bacon and eggs and English muffins ready to cook on an old griddle. I broke several eggs onto the griddle and was about to open the bacon and put the muffins on the grate to toast over the fire when a wet nose nudged my elbow. It didn't just nudge, it forced its way to the front of the griddle. I jumped back to see what this creature was and there were two of the scruffiest, meanest dogs I had ever seen. They did not have friendly eyes and their low growl said I had better not mess with them. I had not seen them in the valley before. They had smelled my fire. They wore no collars and nosed their way right up to the fire, eating my eggs right off the griddle. They gobbled up all the muffins, sniffed around, and disappeared back into the cloud.

I had stepped back against a tree to get out of their way and watched for a minute to see if they were going to come back. They hadn't touched the bacon because the plastic had not yet been sliced open. Their slobber was all over everything. Did they have rabies? Or worse? Suddenly my appetite was gone. I threw everything into a trash bag, put out the fire and went inside the trailer, washed my hands and had a banana and some cookies for breakfast. There had to be good nutrition in there somewhere.

I realized I must have been fortunate that they were primarily interested in my food and not me! Other of my neighbors' dogs and even cats have come over to visit me and we knew each other. I made it a point to befriend all my neighbor's animals so they would get used to my coming over to visit their families. When I mentioned these dogs to the people in the valley, none of them recognized them. They must have come a long way. A thought that occurred to me later was that perhaps those two dogs had belonged to the young man who had been killed by the bear a few years back. With their master gone, they had run off and turned feral.

One lesson I learned from this is not to try to cook a meal outside in the fog. The other lesson would have been to carry my shotgun with me and be more prepared to defend myself. Admittedly that would have been more difficult while trying to cook. The best decision would have been to stay inside during upslope conditions with heavy clouds saturating the hillsides. Now I keep a jar of almond butter and a box of rye crackers with me to be an emergency meal. A can of tuna fish or sardines on crackers works well too. I have since bought a small Coleman two-burner stove which folds up and packs well.

I just have to keep in mind that there are wild things all around and to use common sense about when and where to prepare food. When the fog is out, the wild things get bolder. They smell smoke and food. Just like the enemy, they know I can't see them until they are right there beside me. They come right to my door, waiting to see if I will come out for some reason. So, will I trust the Lord and stay inside to cook and prepare my meals? I have to ask the Lord if it's safe. And He will let me know. "No, Amelia. Wait a bit. Fix your food. Sit down, eat, and spend time with Me. Read awhile and let the danger pass." He has been so good to me. He has saved my life so many times. I can trust Him.

CHAPTER 18

To Live Free or Die

You don't expect to see lions and tigers in the mountains—certainly not leopards and tropical birds. On the way home from town one day, on a whim, I decided to turn off onto a dirt road which beckoned toward the higher elevations.

The tops of the mountains brushed the bottoms of the moody gray clouds and the road headed toward open slopes topped by rocky outcroppings. A fence appeared and then a roof. Around a curve, a barn and then a ranch house came into view. Various outbuildings and sheds were connected with chain link fences.

I pulled into the yard and was about to apologize to a lady for my intrusion, when she said: "Go on in and see the birds."

The birds?

I parked the car and climbed the steps to the cacophony of a massive amount of birds. Entering the living room, I saw all kinds and every size of bird chirping and calling to each other. Dozens of birds, each in its own cage, filled the living and dining rooms. Cockatiels and hawks, bald eagles and parrots, parakeets, canaries and finches; some were obviously injured and were recovering. Others chirped happily as if life was good.

The lady explained that these birds were either found injured or brought here by people who could no longer take care of them and wanted them to be kept safe. Walking around, I listened to the variety of calls and talked to various birds.

As I stepped out the kitchen door into the yard, a strange, deep-throated sound of an unhappy cat reached my ears: a *big* cat. Across the wide parking lot stood some low buildings surrounded by a high chain link fence. I wandered slowly over to investigate this frustrated cry. I knew I shouldn't run toward a wild beast. A yellow and black striped tiger prowled around inside, making everyone else nervous. I started talking to him but he was only interested in complaining.

Across the path from him was an African lion with a dark mane. He made faces and low mutterings as if he had heard it all before. Behind him was a llama in an inaccessible cage.

Walking south along the fence line, I came to a large enclosure. I didn't see anything at first until a tail swished in the grass. As I looked closer, there between a large boulder and the fence lay a huge male lion, his wild mane ruffled up around his head. He appeared to be asleep. As I cautiously walked toward him, I began talking to him in a low calm voice. As I spoke, he raised his head to look at me.

Years ago as a young girl, I used to walk down into the valley to the south, over the railroad tracks, and into the yard of a most interesting farm. This was not a vegetable farm. This was a wild animal farm known as Phifer's Animal Farm. Large circus cages stood around the parking lot containing tigers and other cats being trained. One of these cats had been named Leo. Yes, Leo the Lion—the same lion that's at the beginning of the Metro-Goldwin-Mayer movies. He is now buried on the front lawn of the farm. So I had early experiences with big cats.

Squatting down just outside the fence, I told this lion how beautiful he was. He stared at me as if he were experiencing some new thing. Hadn't anyone spoken to this wild beauty before?

I smiled and continued talking to him for a bit. He seemed to relax as the expression on his face and in his eyes changed. He liked the sound of my voice. Being a massage therapist, I couldn't resist putting my hand on the fence and slowly moving it along the outside. This didn't seem to bother him.

I carefully slipped my fingers through the wires of the fence into his long tawny fur. It was four to five inches of coarse, dusty, thick fur. I felt the deeper layers. My fingers went down to his skin. What a sensation; the sun-warmed skin of a big cat.

Moving my fingers gently on his side, I watched his eyes. Then I slipped my other hand through the wires a few inches away and began massaging with both hands. The strangest thing happened to his eyes, the same look you see when you rub your pet's tummy.

Just then he flopped his head back down and his whole body relaxed. I continued moving my hands in and out between the wires, talking softly, rubbing and scratching his side.

Suddenly I heard the most amazing sound from somewhere deep down in his chest. What was that? My lion was purring! He was permitting me to talk to him and to love him. How incredible! The sound of his purr was like a big "thank you" to my heart. I was almost on the edge of tears. I really didn't want this to end. My lion was at peace.

Then reality hit me that I had food in the car and I had to get home. It was time to say goodbye. I spoke to my lion, telling him how beautiful he was but that I had to go. As I withdrew my fingers, he raised his head, looking at me, still with that contented look in his eyes, but with a touch of "oh, no, don't go" with his mouth slightly open as if he were about to say something.

As I stood to leave, I told him how special he was and that I would see him again.

Turning toward the car, a strange sadness hit me. I turned to look again at my lion. He was still watching me. Silent messages passed between us. He would be okay and I would see him again.

On that drive home back to the old trailer, I realized I had just "made friends" with the king of the beasts, albeit through a fence. Who else that I knew had ever petted a full-grown big cat?

Quietly the revelation came to my heart. I thought… I had been like that lion. I had been in a different kind of cage. My cage was an abusive relationship with nasty, barbed threats, keeping me in, the whip of daily put-downs, things taken away. I would look through the bars at other couples and wonder why we couldn't be that way. So many rules, so many conditions, zero passion or love.

Then I would sense the presence of the Lord. He would speak gently to me. He would reach through the barbs and threats, pushing them aside and walk into the cage and sit with me. He would speak quietly and encourage me. His words gave hope. They shut the angry mouths of accusation and guilt. His presence brought a light that made the bleak hopelessness of darkness flee away. He didn't leave me as I had to leave my lion. He promised that, and He kept His word.

And I purred. From deep down in my spirit, I purred.

CHAPTER 19

The Stories Trees Tell

Today I hiked up to the edge of one of the higher plateaus on my property, about 9570 feet. I sat resting on the stump of an ancient ponderosa pine tree, the sentinel of which had been cut down one hundred years or more ago. The stump still showed its rings; I counted seventy nine of them, but age and weather had worked their way deep down between each ring, the wood dry but amazingly strong. It was like sitting on top of tall flat-topped spikes.

I looked out across my high valley, thinking of the people who had farmed this area back then. They planted potatoes. They built log cabins, some parts of which still stand. They built dugouts, the roofs and front walls supported by logs they had cut and hauled to the site. They built a log community building on the curve of the road. It would have been a quiet life, away from progress, rapidly developing towns, and ranches down below.

When this tree was cut, it was most likely hauled down the hill to be used as part of the wall of a new cabin, possibly the center beam of the house. Part of it might have been made into boards for a door or counters and shelves for the kitchen. Perhaps in the evening, a husband carved a bowl or a cutting board for his wife, a dipper for water, or boards for a wagon or buckboard. None of it would have gone to waste. A wedge held a door open. A few pegs on a wall held clothes, pots and pans, tools.

I thought of my Dad's huge ancient saw that stood in the corner of his garage. It was six feet long with two perpendicular wooden handles, one at each end. It was a two-man saw used to cut down giant trees. I still have it. I never knew him to cut down huge trees. He would have needed help and he never asked me. I spent so much time with Dad when he was home. He was the fixer, the tinkerer. He could make anything work. His garage was like a wonder cave—a room like a giant magician's bag. Pull this knob and find cotter pins, another, lock washers, others, carefully graded screws of all sizes, brads, wire, wing nuts. On the walls hung his beloved tools, in the corner stood the saw.

So the tree left my mountainside to become part of someone's home. Perhaps it became one of the beams holding up the roof over the kitchen and dining table from which hung an oil lamp to light the room. For decades Mom hung a delicate, hand-painted glass oil lamp over our dining table. It was suspended by chains and was hung with dozens of prisms which sparkled around the room. By pushing gently it could be moved closer to the ceiling. By pulling down it would give more light to a meal. I still have it. It's packed away safely, waiting to be hung in my own kitchen or dining room.

I sat on the stump thinking about trees. They are the framework of the landscape. They anchor mountainsides. Their roots go deep into the soil and rocks to stabilize and hold it in place while streams flow by. Trees shelter birds, squirrels, and insects. Their shade comforts us. As a windbreak, they shelter our homes, our fields. Johnny Appleseed knew the value of apple trees.

I thought of the trees I have known. One huge oak tree in the center of town—now over three hundred years old, long limbs propped up by metal pipes—has been cared for by generations of thoughtful people. It amazed me as a girl. It is still standing as far as I know.

Those old trees were standing during the American Revolutionary War. They were standing when the Declaration of Independence was signed. They were standing when Paul Revere took his midnight ride, when Washington crossed the Delaware, when Lincoln emancipated the slaves, when Davy Crockett fought in the battle of the Alamo. They witnessed the covered wagons of the pioneers leaving to cross the plains to build the breadbasket of our country; to build communities, farms and ranches; to dam rivers; to prospect for gold. They were still standing when I was born.

These old trees stand for stability, reminding us of the cost to create this country. No one started out on that trek with just a carpet bag, or a horse pulling a wagon, a milk cow in tow, leaving precious possessions and family behind, without faith; no, not even the prospector hoping to find gold.

When I buy an antique piece of furniture, I know I'm getting old wood that was cut down a hundred to two hundred years ago or more. These are well-made pieces with dovetail joints and fine craftsmanship in maple, oak, cherry, walnut, pine, bird's eye maple. I honor the artisans who took great care and patience to create fine pieces of furniture. No matter which pieces I put together in the same room, they all blend. Each one brings back a memory—an occasion, friends who came to visit, holidays.

The most famous wooden structure in the world was made of gopher wood, which is like cypress, a solid water-resistant wood. Noah built a huge boat four hundred feet long, seventy-five feet high, and forty feet wide. Interestingly, these same proportions have been used in the last century to build our large ocean-going vessels.

The most famous pieces of furniture ever built were made of acacia wood: the base of the Ark of the Covenant with its poles, the mercy seat, the table of showbread, the table of burnt offering. Acacia trees are delicate and gentle in appearance, with a slender trunk, branches flat on the bottom, and a gentle curve around the top.

Each kind of wood fit its use well. King David gathered cedars from Lebanon for the temple that King Solomon built. Later, hundreds of workers cut down those huge trees and King Cyrus shipped them by sea and by land to Jerusalem where the temple was built.

Mom and Dad took care of the trees on their property. They had tall maples along the road above an ancient stone wall. Their home was an old stagecoach stop, schoolhouse, church, and community building that was later remodeled into a two story cottage-style house with a screened in porch on the side and the original fireplace from school days. Curly maple floors had the nail holes still visible from where the desks had been attached to the floor. They loved it at first sight. As the first private owners, they put up a white picket fence and gate. They planted evergreens around the front door, ivy up the chimney, flowers in the window boxes, and tulips along the path, and ringed the house with flowerbeds. Dogwood, sassafras, maple, oak and walnut trees climbed the hillside behind the house and the ground was covered with myrtle. An oak tree, which the students of the school planted sometime around a hundred and fifty and two hundred years ago, is still standing just behind the house by another stone wall. These trees were all trimmed as needed. Orange tiger lilies ran along the opposite bank of the road. We girls never realized what we'd had until we moved away.

Occasionally when we were young, elderly couples would stop by. Keep in mind that at this writing, I am in my early eighties and this was about the mid to late thirties. That could have put their parents back into the late 1800s. They would say, "We went to school here years ago. Our parents went to school here. They owned a farm down over the hill. They planted this oak tree as students and went to church here too." They called it the Old School House. During my sister's and my last visit to the house a number of years ago, the old cement floor to the woodshed and the cement base of the "two-seater" outhouse were still there. We used to jump rope on the woodshed floor.

Now on my own acreage, I am responsible for thousands of trees. A recent survey of standing dead trees showed that I needed to have sixty trees cut down. I will bring someone in to cut down the dead trees. This is not something I could do even with Dad's old two-man saw and a helper. He's probably looking down now praying that I will never use it. These trees will not be wasted. They will be used as fence rails or firewood. Some of my neighbors have built sheds or small carports from their dead trees.

It is also important to clear underlying brush from the forest floor. This is a constant job and one that can be incorporated into walks and hikes around the property. As the ground is cleared, rocks can be gathered into the wheelbarrow and built into low stone walls to define walks and driveways. I have two ridges of moss rock running up my hill. There is something satisfying about building a wall or fence from material on the property.

Aspen trees are considered "nurse trees" for the pines and ponderosas. They grow and establish themselves first and form a protective environment for other trees. If there is a good covering of aspen trees it usually means there is good ground water. I found that to be true when I had my land doused.

The aspens give wonderful shade in summer but in the fall their glory is the golden silver-dollar-sized leaves that turn the mountainsides into gorgeous patchworks of yellow against the deep evergreen of the pines. I know nothing can compare with the colorful display of the mountains in New England in October. But I am here and when the leaves turn, they form a canopy in the shape of a cathedral sixty feet over my head. When they fall I have as much fun running and jumping in them as anyone. I enjoy my trees and they shower me with their golden leaves.

There are two more trees that I need to mention in this chapter. These were the Tree of Life and the Tree of the Knowledge of Good and Evil in the garden of Eden. We will see the Tree of Life in heaven. Adam and Eve could not eat of the Tree of the Knowledge of Good and Evil, lest they die. The fruit of this tree had no visible seeds. Its seeds were spiritual. When the fruit was eaten, the spiritual seeds produced the knowledge of good and evil.

Let me say that it was not an apple tree. No. It couldn't have been and I can prove it! God said that Adam and Eve could eat of any tree that had the seed within the fruit (Genesis 1:29). Apples have seeds. This tree of the Knowledge of Good and Evil was a tree of death! No visible seeds were within its fruit. When a piece of its fruit fell to the ground, no new sapling grew. The two invisible seeds that were within this fruit were the spiritual seeds of the knowledge of good and the knowledge of evil. God warned them. Both Adam and Eve disobeyed. It may have been a beautiful tree, but it was the tree of spiritual death.

CHAPTER 20

The Luxury of Lack

I did not have the luxury of abundance; I had the luxury of lack. I had Walden's without the pond. I was the old woman without the shoe, the carriage without the horse, the piggy without the bank. Nevertheless, if I wanted to survive here, I had to use all the common sense, camping and nature skills I had learned as a child and as a Girl Scout. So, now I was bringing life back from the dead, reviving an old derelict trailer for shelter for a sixty-something woman, bringing new hope to a land that had lain idle for decades.

We learn some things without anyone sitting down and teaching us. One of these things for me was an excellent work ethic. All I had to do was watch my parents!

Dad rose and dressed at six. Mom served him breakfast and drove him to the station to catch the train. His was a twelve hour day. He did that for forty-five years! On weekends he spent time with us girls, worked in the garden, fixed things, took the family on drives out into the country.

During the week mom stayed home and raised us. She was a true homemaker, not going out to work. She cooked meals from scratch. No such thing as "fast food" back then. In fact, she and Dad raised most of our food—fresh vegetables from their one-acre Victory garden, which produced much more than we needed. We girls would take baskets of fresh vegetables—tomatoes, lettuce, cucumbers, spinach, squash, carrots—to the neighbors and sell them for fifty cents. The neighbors loved it. Mom would can the rest. She took us berry picking and we'd come home with buckets of blackberries. We'd drive out to the orchards and have baskets of apples for pie, and peaches, plums, and grapes for jelly and juice. She canned and carefully carried them down to the cellar and placed them on the shelves of the canning room Dad had built for her.

They really worked well together. He was so proud of her. They had a household of bounty. We were never short of food to serve to our guests.

So in order to survive, I had to pretend the trailer was a tent with solid walls. I replaced the broken door with a steel one that would keep out bears and other hungry animals. With no electricity, I used a plastic picnic ice chest that sat on the kitchen floor. Three times a week I drove to the country store for a block of ice. I purchased inexpensive oil lamps and bottles of lamp oil so I could read at night. I carried water home from various neighbor's wells in eight two-gallon jugs. I purchased firewood on the way home from shopping in the city. I could pile about half a cord in the back of my pickup. The woodstove in the trailer served as my cook stove, hot water heater, furnace, and my clothes dryer on rainy days. Some of my friends started calling me "Mrs. Lincoln." Yes, I did split my own wood and gathered sticks and branches for tinder and saved newspapers for starting the fire. I watched how my neighbors did things. I asked questions and they were glad to answer.

Two things impressed me about my neighbors. Each one seemed to have a different unique ability that the others needed. One gave riding lessons. Another could build concrete block buildings and barns. One could weld. Another built solar installations to power homes. Several designed and built log homes. Somebody owned heavy equipment which could be used to dig foundations, basements, and driveways. Many put up their own fences, which is hard work. One could find water on the land by dousing. Some built greenhouses. Others knew how to raise chickens.

The second thing that impressed me was the sense of community throughout the valley. If someone needed help, one or more people would stop by and figure out the problem.

I was on my way down the mountain one day when I noticed my truck was leaving a dark trail of liquid on the road. I had just pulled over, gotten out to take a look and popped open my hood when a neighbor's truck pulled up beside me. Without saying anything, she got out of her vehicle, looked at my engine, and walked back along the road tracking the liquid. She said, "You've been losing radiator fluid. I spotted it on the road back a ways. You'll be all right. Just pick up a couple of gallons of antifreeze as soon as you get to the store. Let the engine cool down and refill your radiator. You'll be fine. You're almost there." Amazed, I thanked her as she got into her truck and drove away.

The sense of community was reinforced by neighbors who loved to cook. One woman would call another and say, "I'm cooking a roast today. Bring a salad and come to dinner. My neighbor is bringing a pie. Call your neighbors and invite them. Ask them to bring some bread and butter." The word went out and four or five families would gather for an impromptu meal. This could happen two or three times a week, always at a different house. People truly are more important than things.

Why fear lack when necessity is the mother of invention? Do we fear lack just because we're so used to plenty? I have learned with the apostle Paul to abound and to be abased, to be content. I have experienced a "mountain high" just being able to solve some problem myself that I would never have encountered back in the city. Is what we have really lack or laziness? Is it lack, or fear, lack, or opportunity? Perhaps there is a better definition. Is it really lack when we have all the basic things to support life just as our ancestors did two hundred, three hundred, two thousand, three thousand years ago? Living on a homestead, I quickly rejected a "tin cup" attitude which says the world owes me this or that. I considered how many times Abraham, Isaac, and Jacob had to start over, dig another well and another. If I lack all the gadgets and unnecessary toys considered essential, the electronic conveniences which have made us lazy, does this indicate I lack the ability to live a meaningful life? If we lack the high-powered vehicles to take us places, this does not mean our lives are limited or less enjoyable. We don't really need them now. We trade the gym for the path. We must depend more upon our legs to get us around. Our communities become smaller, more intimate, more attuned to other's needs.

We learn to work together, help each other, barter. We go back to what's important, what the older generations learned: respect, honesty, truth, where a man's word was his bond. Neighbor helping neighbor.

Without TV or the stereo system, it's suddenly quiet. We can hear God. We have time to think on godly things. While we are hand washing our clothes we can be thankful we have water. We can hum a tune, sing songs to Him. In our home while I was growing up, my mother sang songs around the house. She taught me how to count in French. I would repeat after her. I would hum or whistle. I would imitate the birds. My dad had a happy countenance. One of his favorite things to do was to fix something, finding satisfaction in making something work better.

I remember as a girl seeing Dad go out the back door in his bathrobe and slippers, while Mom fixed breakfast, with a bag of sunflower seeds in his hand. We lived next to the woods and an old stone wall ran behind the house. In this stone wall lived a family of chipmunks. They would hear him coming and run scampering to him waiting for him to open the bag. He would reach in the bag and pull out a handful of seeds, placing some seeds on the toes of his slippers. Immediately they were up on his slippers, sitting and eating the seeds. Such simple things to bring delight.

While we split wood, we can be thankful for the exercise and fresh air, thankful for the woodstove that heats our home. Hanging wash on the line, we can be thankful for saving the environment, not using power to dry our clothes.

Not having conveniences forces us to be in and out of our homes many times a day. We are continually getting exercise. Outside we are cultivating a garden, pulling weeds, planting seeds, sweeping the steps and path, taking time to sit down on a bench and enjoy the sun.

Don't have a bench? We would build one out of whatever we had: a log, or two short lengths of unsplit firewood and a plank. You get the idea.

A wheelbarrow is a wonderful investment, particularly if a person has rocks to clear away. They can be used to build a stone wall, perhaps at the entry of the driveway or around the garden.

In the mountains a greenhouse is necessary, yes, but also at lower altitudes a greenhouse will protect produce from deer, raccoons, bear and birds. Let me describe a greenhouse built by one of my neighbors.

It was a geodesic dome that he built with the help of his neighbors, and he shared his produce with them. He made it with two-by-four triangles fitted with double layer insulated clear plastic panels. Several of these opened around the top. These were opened and closed morning and evening automatically by heat sensitive hinges that responded to the sun. This enabled the bees to enter and pollinate the plants, eliminating hand pollination. The dome was thirty-five feet in diameter. It was built on a two-foot deep footing. Around the inside of the dome he built a raised bed about two feet wide. In the center was another raised bed with a gravel path circling between the beds. On the north side he installed an oval stock tank that he filled with water. Over the top of the tank he laid a sturdy wood grate on which he put potted plants. The water in the tank absorbed heat during the day and released it at night, moderating the temperature and the humidity.

Under the entire dirt floor, about one foot down, a four-inch black plastic flexible hose ran back and forth, one end of which was carried up the back wall to the top of the dome. In the very top of this hose, he installed a small fan powered with a solar panel which automatically turned on as the sun rose. The top of the dome was a perfect collection spot for heat during the day. This heat was forced down through the underground hose all day to heat the soil of the greenhouse and keep the ground warm at night. Temperatures at night in the mountains can go below freezing. His system worked so well it was like walking into a jungle. His tomato plants were higher than I could reach. The aroma of fresh herbs was wonderful. Working in a greenhouse for an hour or two a day gives the system a tremendous boost of oxygen, a definite plus at higher altitudes. Having a greenhouse is another dream of mine.

Not having everything one needs reinforces the idea of figuring out a problem alone. To figure out most problems, you don't need to be a rocket scientist. Our forefathers in the 1600s and 1700s never had the advanced education we have today, yet they built this country with common sense and faith in God, common law, and county rule.

The abundance of lack always exists in a homesteading situation. Whether people had a carpet bag, a milk cow, or just a tent, they had to figure out from day one how they were going to survive. If they were rich enough to have a saw and draw knife, they were rich enough to build themselves a log cabin. They were also rich enough to start a business helping others build their own homes.

I have Dad's antique draw knife with me in the trailer. It's a two-handled knife used to shave surfaces. My son Josh plans to use it to try his hand at removing the bark from some of the aspen trees that have blown over. He is very creative. We will see what he is able to with these trees.

Ah, so now we come to the real luxury of lack, when all else fails. What if we no longer had a place to stay "on the side of a mountain"? We no longer have a tent. We no longer have food, water, fire. What then? Where do we go? Just like the prophets of old, we are then totally in the hands of the Lord. In essence, He told Elijah, "Go to the brook Cherith and I will command the ravens to feed you." When the brook dried up, He sent him to the widow in Zarephath where He told him to ask her to bake a cake for him. Each time he was provided for, and so was the widow, until the end of the famine. (See 1 Kings 17:3–15).

Are we not the bride of Christ and as such are the seed of Abraham through the blood of Christ? As our Bridegroom, Jesus left us with His promises which are "Yea and Amen." As the bride of Christ, each of us is seated with Christ in heavenly places. We have chosen the kingdom of God and have put Him first. We are right now ruling and reigning with Him. We are operating in the kingdom of heaven. Whenever we pray the Lord's Prayer, we pray, "Our Father which art in heaven, hallowed be Thy name. Thy kingdom come. Thy will be done in earth, as it is in heaven." So He has given us the authority to move within the kingdom of heaven. This is so much different than the kingdom of this world where evil reigns, sickness and failure rule.

The prophets knew how to operate and live in the kingdom of heaven and Jesus taught his followers to walk there also. When He sent out the seventy, they came back rejoicing that even the demons were subject to them in Jesus' name. How did they operate in the kingdom of heaven? This was not just for "back then" but for today. I have a choice. Either I operate in the kingdom of this world or I operate in the kingdom of heaven. If I chose to operate in the kingdom of heaven, then things of this world no longer control me. I have given up debt and overcome the need to have things everyone else has. I have chosen the kingdom of God and have put Him first in my life. I no longer have to "keep up with the Joneses." Besides, the Joneses have huge mortgages and businesses that take much time away from their family, so the quality of life is diminished.

As we walk about the countryside under the direction of the Holy Spirit, we will be taken care of as we pray for others. Is there any sick among you? Call for the elders and anoint the person with oil. It's a long way to any doctor. A simple prayer: "In the name of Jesus, be healed." "Rise up and walk!" "Spine, come into line!" Ezekiel 16:6 says, "When I passed by thee, and saw thee polluted in thine own blood, I said unto thee … Live!" The prayer of faith shall heal them. The kingdom of heaven is all about trust. We trust God's Word.

We all will have come full circle back to the first century. We will be more perfectly healed than any doctor can perform and without the high cost. We have God's 911. Psalm 91:1 says: "He that dwelleth in the secret place of the most High shall abide under the shadow of the Almighty."

With God we will lack nothing. His angels are ministering spirits given to minister to us, protect us, fight demonic powers, and, as I found out, surround our homes in times of danger. They kept me alive in a deadly car wreck that demolished my Toyota Land Cruiser. They kept our four-year-old son Josh from falling out of the car as the passenger door inexplicably swung open when we were traveling at seventy-five miles per hour on the freeway. This was years before baby seats and safety belts. I reached over and grabbed his arm as I pulled over to the side of the road. He never even looked out the open door! I went around the car and locked and shut the door. Then I sat there thanking the Lord for holding onto my son! Today he and his older brother Mike are the strong arrows in my quiver (Psalm 127:3–5). Faith is all about trust in His Word because He holds His Word above His name to perform it.

Amen.

CHAPTER 21

The Art of Waiting

Remember that young girl wandering around the woods, learning about life? Little did I know what was in my future. As I grew I learned about God, about people in the world who didn't know about Him. I yearned to be a missionary, to be able to tell them about His Love for them. When I told my desire to my parents, they emphatically said, "No.". Even highly respected people told me, "No." So the desire of my heart was derailed. I was sent away to school to study a more acceptable profession: Sociology.

Theoretically, as a sociologist I would be able to help people here at home. My studies did not go well. My heart was not in it. My professors knew it. I decided to follow my second choice and use my scholarship to art school. I did very well. I loved it. I was perfecting my skills. Then, I received a proposal of marriage. He was well educated, had a good job, was polite, a gentleman, I thought, and my parents approved.

After the wedding, things changed immediately. I was told to get a job. I realized I had married a man whom I hardly knew. Now I had the job ahead of me of telling him about the love of God. In a strange twist of fate, my life as a real missionary had begun. The children came and grew. My husband made a profession of faith. Each child came to know the Lord. Relatives, cousins, uncles, nieces, nephews, in-laws, over the years, came to profess Jesus as Lord. They all grew. They matured. I watched lives struggle, rejoice in new babies, go off to school, work out hard problems, go through the deaths of loved ones, watch grandchildren grow, new children discover life! And then, after years of abuse that continued right up to the end, I knew I had to go. He hadn't wanted me for a while. I had to forgive him and I had to let go. I had to start over and build a new life. And thus I ended up on the side of a mountain.

Did my house ever get built? Absolutely. Can you see it if you go there today? Only if I go with you. Why? It isn't a visible house. It wasn't built with human hands. The foundation is solid rock, built on The Lord Jesus Christ, Yeshua Ha Meshiach, His Hebrew name.

Board upon board, plank upon plank it was built, beginning with the strength to leave a situation that couldn't be resolved. There was the huge plank of trust that God would take care of me plus the plank of the knowledge of His Word, that he would supply all my needs according to His riches in glory by Christ Jesus. The nails are there (ouch) of learning the hard way to obey the Word and not start out marriage unequally yoked with an unbeliever. The comfort here is that my husband did come to believe in the Lord.

There was the great pain of the saw cutting through planks previously built on lies needing to be removed. The pain and hurting of my children, which has been long in mending, being dovetailed and carefully glued back in place making a stronger bond than before as finally understanding and forgiveness grows.

There was the strength and adventure of deciding to live outside the box of what people thought I should do. The decision to live on my land in a remote area was not what many people would have chosen. I knew I was blessed to have the land. I had dreams of homesteading but not the means. That required the beam of determination that existence was possible whether other people thought so or not, even if a house was never built. I know my friends worried about me. Some called me "Mrs. Lincoln". They laughed when they said it but I took it as a compliment. That would be quite a name to live up to. This life would require the planning of simple ways I could make the trailer safe for me and for my cats from roaming bears, pack rats, coyotes, owls, cougar, using common sense, bringing them inside at sunset when the prowlers were about and not going out myself after dark before making sure the glen was clear of them.

There was the plank of education, learning about homesteading, learning where there might be water, learning the contours of my land, locating the best building spots, to be ready if it were ever possible to begin building my dream.

There was the humor, inventiveness and generosity of my neighbors, learning how they handled their problems, which was a major plank in my life. The bright sparkling nail in one of the boards of provision was that I was eventually able to have phone service directly to my trailer because some of my neighbors needed phones. The old phone line still runs along the ground from the original post that I imagined the pack rat would climb. Still no cell phone towers in the valley. Thank goodness!

I learned the mountain way of bartering which enabled me to have a driveway, an erosion control dam, a Servel gas refrigerator and a used solar system. Years ago the Servel gas refrigerator was the mainstay of many homes. They are actually still being made.

The roof of my spiritual home was built as I experienced a ferocious mountain storm, alone, without the protection of lightning rods and with only my prayers and trust that God would protect me. The walls of appreciation rose as I was forced to use primitive means of lighting my home with oil lamps. Not having running water forced me to humble myself to go to some of my neighbors and ask for water from their wells.

Strengthening joists in the floor came about because of a good work ethic, not pulling away from a tough job, the choice of getting out there and splitting wood or being cold in the evenings.

There was the plank of keeping healthy, active, taking care of small health problems before they became major, making use of what I had and finding simple solutions, easy ways to prepare meals, soups, stews to give me energy.

The planks of prayer and trust were right there supporting the plank of planning what I would have to do if I had an accident, how I would get help, which neighbor I could go to or call in an emergency. They stood in the doorway as the threshold, lintels and doorposts.

There is the attitude of humility and wonder in my life as I consider all the Lord has brought me through. What is lacking is the spirit of independence, the "I can do anything" attitude. I was a different kind of pilgrim. I came into His rest. I was testing spiritual waters as I searched for physical water on my land. I was plowing the soil, preparing it for others coming after me who might want to know the way to build their own houses with fear and trembling but learning not to fear the things coming upon the earth, but to trust the Maker.

They are out there, those who might want to find what I have found. They will need to know that the way is difficult, that it takes faith, determination, patience, seeking His Face, the inner strength He gives you through His joy, allowing Him the freedom to build, reconstruct where necessary, learn new things to you that are very old, things that go back to our Judeo-Christian roots. They will need to search for old planks, barn wood, that has been around for generations, planks soaked in the rains of truth, drenched with the lives of the Prophets and the Sages, held together with Psalms and hymns and spiritual songs, with the teachings of Solomon and Job, Ruth and Ester, and the lessons of Adam and Eve, Sampson, Thomas, and Stephen, and giving honor to our great Fathers, Abraham, Isaac and Jacob. Walk along life's driveway with Peter and Paul. They stumbled and fell but they got up and moved in the brilliant power of the Holy Spirit and built the Church in the power of the Name of Jesus - Yeshua. I can recommend them as excellent contractors for a life built on truth, on the Rock of our salvation.

When you come by to visit you will find the windows of my spiritual house are polished with the light of His wisdom which He put there. The food in my kitchen is simple but nutritious, the Bread of Life, the manna He has promised in the wilderness. My pantry is full of the Word, a rich storehouse which I can share anytime. My door is always open in welcome to whomever wants to build their house on the Rock, and it is the Spirit Who draws us into His Love.

So, come, sit with me on my log. There's plenty of room, and we'll talk and have a piece of that bread.

SECTION 3
The End of the Roll

Survival Tips for Pilgrims

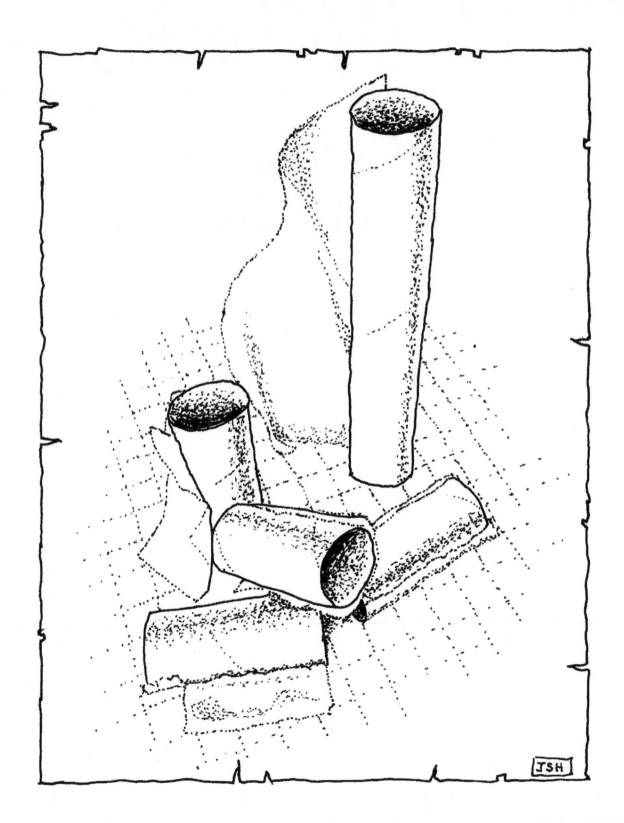

CHAPTER 22

When the Paper Runs Out

While living in the derelict trailer, I clearly realized the waste of so many paper products and the irresponsible ways we use water. We make fun of stories our great grandparents told of making sure there was always a copy of the Montgomery Ward or other catalogs in the outhouse. That was the way of life back then. There was no such thing as toilet paper, paper towels, tissues—things we take for granted nowadays and throw away. Worn-out clothes were cut up and made into warm patchwork quilts or cut down into smaller sizes for younger children. People didn't throw things away but reused them for other purposes. Fancy laces were carefully removed from worn-out dresses and put away to be used on other dresses later. Material from the dresses was made into aprons, bonnets, or small purses.

In the trailer, I had both paper towels and terrycloth towels for everyday use in the kitchen, but found myself letting the paper towels dry on the dish rack between meals and reusing them several times during the day. I was also careful about how many terrycloth towels I used as I had to hand wash them every week.

The one place in which I was most efficient was the conservative use of water. It was necessary to haul water in twice a week from various neighbor's wells and I could only get thirty-two gallons each week, a little more than the size of the average hot water heater. I learned quickly how to consistently use water wisely. As stated in the chapter on water, I learned to bathe using a large stainless steel bowl similar in size to the old-fashioned ceramic bowls and pitchers used generations ago. This used only about four cups of water. My water was hot as opposed to the cold water which sat in the pitcher on our ancestors' washstand all night. Also, twice a week I took a shower using a camping sun shower with two-and-a-half gallons of hot water, heated on my woodstove, which was enough to bathe, shampoo, and rinse my hair. I woke up my face in the mornings by dipping a pan into the large pot of steaming water on the woodstove and using that to wash my face.

Washing two loads of clothes by hand still left enough water for drinking and cooking and the left over dishwater was used to clean counters, floors and bathroom with the addition of some extra bleach. Cleaning is speeded up by putting three parts water and one part vinegar in a spray bottle. Or try one cup water and one or two tablespoons bleach in a spray bottle for vinyl floors. Do not mix these solutions.

Decades ago, Mom would set a large oval copper boiler half filled with water on two burners of the stove, which she brought to a boil. After washing and bleaching the sheets, handkerchiefs and underwear, she would run them through the ringer on her washing machine and put the sheets and all right into the copper boiler on the stove. She then used a wash club to move the sheets around in the boiler. She lifted the steaming sheets back into the empty washing machine and ran them through the ringer again. Using the wash club, she carried each sheet outside and hung it on the line. She did this in every kind of weather. In the winter, the sheets froze almost instantly, but they dried. The handkerchiefs and underwear went into the laundry basket to be carried out and hung on the line. I still have an old ringer washing machine, illustrated at the beginning of the Waterworks chapter.

Women used these age-old methods to sterilize sheets, handkerchiefs, and underwear every washday. Another way they sanitized their laundry after it was dry was to iron it. Mom had a shaker bottle with a sprinkler head with which she dampened all the starched clothes, shirts, and handkerchiefs. Then she rolled them up and placed them in a pillow case overnight. The next morning she would iron it all.

My daughter Ana, gave me a neat hint years ago about making my own starch. Pour one cup water into a measuring cup. Add one heaping tablespoon cornstarch. Stir until dissolved. Pour through a strainer into a spray bottle. Shake the spray bottle regularly. To keep the starch fresh longer, add a tablespoon of colloidal silver to the container. Spray on shirts and other garments before you iron. Even today, not everyone has a clothes dryer, so this is a simple solution. I have used this idea for years. It has saved money and trips to the store for spray starch.

As I thought through different ways to be conservative with the use of paper products, I began experimenting on ways to eliminate paper entirely. Yes, even thick catalogs. I looked for a material that was soft and absorbent. At a fabric shop, I homed in on white fabric and decided on flannel. It is soft, absorbent, and bleachable. I bought several yards. Choose the kind of fabric that works well for you.

Another source of flannel is resale or second hand shops. They have racks of regular and flannel sheets, quilts, towels, and so on. You can also use old pajamas and nightgowns. Don't forget the scrap bag of material you have left over from all your sewing projects.

I used long strips of toilet paper as a pattern and cut it into two sheet lengths with pinking shears. Recently my sister, Beth, gave me a quilting rotary cutter, eliminating the need for scissors, and now I can cut through five to six layers at one time.

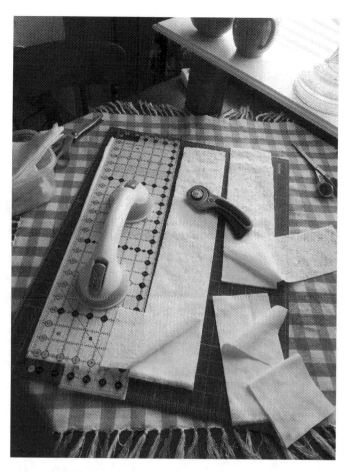

I also cut out handkerchief-sized pieces and used them on a daily basis. I found that the cheaper flannel works best and feels soft on the nose. You can customize the size to suit yourself. These can be kept in a dresser drawer and washed with your regular light clothes. Expect extra lint when drying. Bright dress or shirting material can also be used to coordinate with an outfit. Men's handkerchiefs out of shirting material look quite sharp and these can be hemmed with the newer machines.

After using the flannel "toilet paper," *do not flush* these fabric sheets down the toilet! Place them in a plastic container with a pop-up lid. A large plastic cereal container works well. Put three quarts to one gallon of water and one cup white vinegar in the container. Vinegar deodorizes, kills germs and bacteria, and neutralizes the acid of urine. The lid can be popped closed right away. The flannel will soak so debris is loosened, allowing it to go to the bottom of the container. Then the dirty water is drained down the toilet and the flannel pieces are washed and bleached. This is the same system used by our great-grandmothers generations ago to clean fabric baby diapers. Expect extra lint. This container needs to be a "dedicated" container, used only for this purpose.

Flannel towels cut in the popular half-sheet paper towel size fold well and can be stored in a drawer, stacked on the counter, or stored in a pop-lid plastic box. I keep mine just inside an upper cabinet door, yes even now. These can be washed with the regular light clothes or towels. They can also be hung over a rack to dry between uses. These sheets can be used to dust and polish furniture, to clean up highchairs and other spills, in the bathroom to clean sinks, and so on. Keep some in a bag in the car to clean up spills. Spray with colloidal silver water to clean sticky hands.

Next on my list were the moist feminine wipes purchased in small plastic boxes. I used the same size as the double-sheet toilet paper, so cutting all these at the same time was easy. After I cut these sheets, I folded them accordion style into each other, placed them in the small plastic boxes with a mixture of ¼ cup water and ¼ cup witch hazel. I threaded the top sheet through the slot and shut the lid. After use, put these wipes into the same container with the recyclable "toilet paper." Another option is to use a small travel size spray bottle of colloidal-silver water and spray a small clean piece of flannel just before use. Process it the same way. Health food stores carry small blue glass or amber glass spray bottles which can fit into a purse.

A tiny, single, three-inch by three-inch sheet size of flannel folded can be placed in the area of the hemorrhoids for comfort. These can be placed in a snack sized plastic bag to which can be added approximately ¼ cup witch hazel. Any excess liquid should be pressed out. After the snack bag is shut, this bag can be slipped into a pocket or purse for future use.

Sanitary napkins can be fashioned with half a dozen toilet-paper sized sheets with a tissue-sized sheet wrapped around and pinned underneath. Perhaps you can get even more creative, using clear packing tape on the bottom for homemade "leak-proof" pads. Generations ago these pads were pinned to thin elastic belts worn beneath the underwear.

Don't forget, most of these suggestions were the way people managed one to two hundred years ago, back when people had real fabric baby diapers and fabric sanitary napkins. Before disposables, this was the normal way of life.

One thing I realize about this new way of thinking is that people will not voluntarily prepare these items, unless they absolutely have to when the emergency arrives. For this reason, I suggest you set aside time to just make up five boxes or containers of these items: one box of thirty or forty cut sheets of the fabric toilet paper and place it in one of the bathroom cabinets, one box of about twenty fabric half-sheets of paper towels and place it in a kitchen cabinet, one or more boxes of the flannel or printed dress or shirt fabric "tissues"/handkerchiefs, and place them in dresser drawers or on the kitchen counter, several small snack size zipper bags of about sixteen of the three inch flannel squares for the hemorrhoid area. These can be placed in purses, knapsacks or travel gear. Then, find a tall, thin plastic cereal box with a plastic cover that has a pop-up lid and place it next to your toilet. This can be filled now with the vinegar/water mixture or you can wait until emergency conditions arrive placing it into one of your lower cabinets in the bathroom for future use. Remember, you won't be alone. This will be a new way of life for those of us who prepare. When emergency situations happen, you may need to leave the house, and you can grab any of these boxes to take with you. There will be no toilet paper in any of the public restrooms, service stations, etc. As you have time you can make up more boxes and put them away.

A simple tooth powder, made of a half-and-half mixture of salt and baking soda, does a wonderful job of cleaning and refreshing teeth and mouth. Keep tooth powder in a small covered glass bowl to keep it dry and fresh. This mixture of salt and soda also makes an excellent gargle which I have used numerous times, to relieve a sore throat. I do a final rinse with pure colloidal silver water.

Vinegar also makes an effective deodorant which I have used for quite a while. Fill a small spray bottle with white vinegar. As mentioned above, vinegar kills germs and bacteria. You don't smell the vinegar after it dries. No guarantee goes with this suggestion as to length of protection. This is not an antiperspirant. When all else fails, soap and water always work well.

Regardless of where we live, it should go without saying that we need to be responsible for our own health and the health of our family. Common sense says we dress appropriately for the weather. If we fall and injure ourselves, we clean a cut or wound and protect it with a bandage or suitable covering while it heals.

Snake bites, tick bites, spider bites, and animal bites need immediate attention. A trip to the doctor or emergency room is necessary.

My son put together a simple colloidal silver generator. He wired three nine-volt batteries together, in-series, and ran wires with alligator clips to two silver wires that were suspended in a quart jar of water. He let this sit for about ten to fifteen minutes. He could see a "mist" coming off one wire and bubbles coming off the other wire. He kept the colloidal silver water in a glass jar. He used it along with other over-the-counter products to help fight a nasty stomach flu. This is a project that anyone can do in thirty minutes or less. Fittings for connecting nine-volt batteries can be found in a hardware store. Yes, even a great-grandma like me can do this. It could be a fun afternoon project for any family.

Colloidal silver has been used to fight germs since the late 1800s. It was used as an antiseptic and an antibiotic on a regular basis for illness until penicillin came into use along with other antibiotics in the 1930s and 1940s. Before that, the wealthy got the necessary amount of silver into their diets by using real silverware and eating on silver platters. In colonial days and before, farmers used to hang a silver spoon in the water tank in the farm yard to keep the water fresh for the animals. Silver kills germs and bacteria. Today, doctors put silver mesh on serious wounds to kill germs and to hasten healing.

I have found that when I take colloidal silver, I also need to take a probiotic at the opposite end of the day.

CHAPTER 23

Serious Survival Suggestions

L et's imagine that you or someone close to you may at some time in the future be in a situation where you have to survive. You may have a piece of land, or a friend's cabin that you might borrow for a period of time. Perhaps you have your own cabin where you go on vacation. You may have to make do right in your home without power.

This is a country of campers and outdoorsmen. We love to be outside and we have all sorts of camping equipment. We hike, fish, hunt. Many of us have gone rafting down different rivers. The road to the top of the mountain always beckons. We ask ourselves, "Where does it end? Does it go to the other side or does it end in a cave? Did I bring my pan in case I want to pan for gold? Do I know this trail well enough to hike it by myself? Am I prepared for emergencies if the weather turns ugly? Do I have my survival pack?"

These are all short-term situations. You may have to consider how to take care of yourself for weeks or months. Would you be roughing it alone or with members of your family? Do you have young children, pets? How will they fare if everything were to stop today as you know it? This is where preplanning really pays. It removes a lot of the fear.

A solid roof over your head is better than a tent. A trailer is better than a tent. We've all heard stories of wild animals getting bolder and bolder, less afraid of humans. We've seen newscasts of the bear that got into an office building and went right to the refrigerator in the kitchen area and cleaned it out. And then he left! How did he know? We've taught them.

Small animals disappear. I've lost a cat to coyotes. When an owl flew through the glen, if I had not been standing out there waving him off, I might have lost another cat that evening.

We've heard stories of wild animals such as panthers, tigers, snakes brought from other countries to be pets and later abandoned in the woods to grow up wild and become deadly predators. These animals are still out there. They are not cute little pets anymore. They are hungry and smart. You really don't want one of those pawing its way into your tent or camper.

Bears are not cute. They are not teddy bears. They are deadly. You don't play with them. You don't feed them. You don't let your children follow them. Buffalo are even worse. Even though they are on our buffalo nickels, this doesn't make them nice or pet-able. They have gored people. It takes a very strong fence to contain a buffalo. Keep your distance.

Understood.

Keep your food in a safe place. Use metal lockers when possible. Have a bear rope you can use to hoist your food into a tree or between two trees. Yes, bears can climb trees, but you're not making it easy for them.

I came home from work one night to find a yearling bear cub browsing next to my trailer. The sound of my engine scared him away. I did not care to know if the mother was around. I got into the trailer as quickly as possible, locked my door, and lit my oil lamps and made sure I knew where my shotgun was.

Be smart. Consider your options carefully. What do you have? Can you trade what you have for an upgrade—an all-season camper, trailer, or motor home? Now is the time to find what you or your family need, before you need it. Learn how to use it.

I remember as a Girl Scout making up a bedroll out of blankets and scouting around the area for twigs, small logs or tinder to make a fire. We learned to be responsible. We learned simple chores that would be needed in a camp, like gathering stones to make a fire ring to contain a fire, setting up a simple kitchen, erecting a tarp to keep things and people dry, tying two crook sticks together with wire to form a hook to hang a pot over the fire. We were taught to carry these items in our backpacks: flashlights; toothbrush and toothpaste; several extra pair of socks; clean underwear; extra pants; shirts; sweatshirts; comb; our Girl Scout handbooks and other books; a Bible; chocolate bars for s'mores over the fire; some small games; cards; a small box of matches which had been dipped in candle wax for waterproofing; trash bags; and raincoat; plus a canteen of water over our shoulder. Today that would be adjusted to a cigarette lighter, snack bars, a cell phone. Each person should be responsible for his or her own bag and know where it is kept.

I remember during the Second World War, when we girls were young, the town would have air raid drills. Dad was an air raid warden. The sirens would blow. We knew the drill:

- Throw heavy blankets over the windows.
- Push the dining room table against the wall.
- Cover the table with blankets.
- Put water, crackers and pillows under the table.
- Take cover under the table and stay there until the "all clear" sounded.

Dad would check on us to make sure we did it right.

We painted the top half of our car headlights with black paint to be less visible from the air.

We each had our own flashlights and canteens. We were scouts. We also had a cellar, like most of the older houses, where we would go if we needed another place of safety.

One thing I learned living on the mountain was to buy good tools, the best I could afford. Then I learned not to loan them out or they might not be returned. Or if they were returned it might not be the same tool I loaned out but an older one, somebody else's tool. I solved this problem by making it a policy to never loan out my tools. If someone needed help I would go with my tools, use them to help, and bring my tools home with me when I was done.

In my situation, survival meant having enough firewood for cooking and to heat the trailer at night, all night. I had plenty of blankets and a down comforter on my bed. Usually the trailer maintained enough residual heat to be reasonably comfortable until the morning. However, this did not always work out. Mountain temperatures get below freezing at night, particularly at ninety five hundred feet. Children or seniors cannot stand these cold temperatures. .

Experience has taught me that it is a necessity, especially for children and the elderly in a primitive situation, for each person to have two hot water bottles at night, one for the feet and the other in the tummy area to keep up the core temperature. If no hot water bottles are available, pint or quart canning jars can be used. Wrap these in small towels or place them in homemade cases made of towels that button at the top. These can be placed in the bed fifteen or twenty minutes before going to bed just like an old fashioned bed warmer. It may be necessary to replenish the hot water halfway through the night. Keep the pot of water going on the stove. By the way, this water can be used over and over, simply reheating it in a separate pan. Recycled water; what a concept!

An excellent first aid kit should be a part of any family campout. Any camping supply store should have well stocked kits. You just have to make sure you have more of everything for a longer stay. If you know CPR, great; if not, take a course now.

Know how to make a travois in case you're out away from your camp and someone gets injured. You will need a small hatchet, a blanket, and rope. Cut down two small trees at least two to three inches thick. The trees will have to be strong and heavy enough to carry a two-hundred-pound person and about twelve to fifteen feet long. Young aspen trees would work well. Wrap the blanket around the poles by rolling the poles inward toward each other. Flip the travois over so that the taut part of the blanket is on top. Secure the blanket at each corner with the rope, using a shorter stretch of rope between the foot end than at the head end. The ends of the travois will drag along the ground and need to be closer together.

It might be easier to pre-make a travois sling that can fit into a backpack. This can be made out of heavy canvas cut in a long trapezoidal shape with the top about twenty-four to thirty inches wide, the foot about eighteen to twenty inches wide, and the length about six to seven feet. Hem the edges with double seams and put grommets along these edges. The rope you carry can be threaded through these and around the two tree trunks.

Heavy leather work gloves are a must and another pair of gloves for warmth. Carry extra pairs with you. Children need to keep their hands warm, especially in the evenings. If anyone in the family knits, a good project would be warm socks and gloves or mittens. Mittens are warmer.

Some campsites might have washing machines and dryers. In a more primitive situation, washing clothes by hand as I did would require the rationing of water, the use of a washboard in a tub, conserving soap, using a small amount of bleach, and hanging the wash on a line between two or three trees. A notched pole can prop up a heavy line to keep clothes off the ground. A laundry basket is essential for sorting laundry and carrying it to the line. Make sure you have a backup line in case one line breaks. Clothespins can be used for other things like pinning curtains back or together, keeping bags of chips shut, clipping mail together, keeping notes organized.

Ideally it would be nice to have a camp kitchen. A home project for the family could be to design and build a plywood kitchen with one long side which would fold down into a wide work surface, storage compartments, cubbyholes, hooks to hang utensils, and sturdy legs. Don't leave Mom out in designing this. You can get all sorts of ideas from camping books and magazines.

Teach your children and teens how to safely build campfires and how to cook simple things. Guide them in how to use a cigarette lighter correctly to start a cook fire. Do not let the younger children keep it between meals. Cigarette lighters and matches are not toys. Stress safety and conservation. Monitor them. Make camping fun for them.

Give kids projects to do around camp. Let them make their own walking sticks. This could take some time with carving initials, decorative designs, symbols. .

Make sure each child has a whistle. Three blows means "help." Don't let them blow the whistle in each other's ears! Practice the buddy system. Never go anywhere by yourself!

Teach children how to use a compass.

Black plastic garbage bags can be a raincoat.

Label drinking cups with names.

Use bandanas around necks and, when wet, as smoke masks.

Canteens go everywhere.

A compass gets you home.

Take cell phone pictures: you don't need cell phone reception to take pictures. If you have a generator, these can be recharged. Get a pocket battery charger for your family.

Don't get close to a wild animal. Stand still. You cannot outrun a bear! This is why you need the buddy system.

The things girls need … yes!

Do not take girls or women hiking during their periods! This attracts bears. Keep them in the camp close to protection and other family members.

Have older siblings watch over younger ones. This is no time for horsing around or teasing. This is the time young men learn responsibility, to grow up. Are there scouts in the family? This is the time for them to show exactly what they've learned. Work together. Take care of each other. Be considerate. Love each other. Love will cast out fear and cover a multitude of sins. Remember, you are living in the Kingdom of God now. I found all these things worked for me while I was living on the side of my mountain.

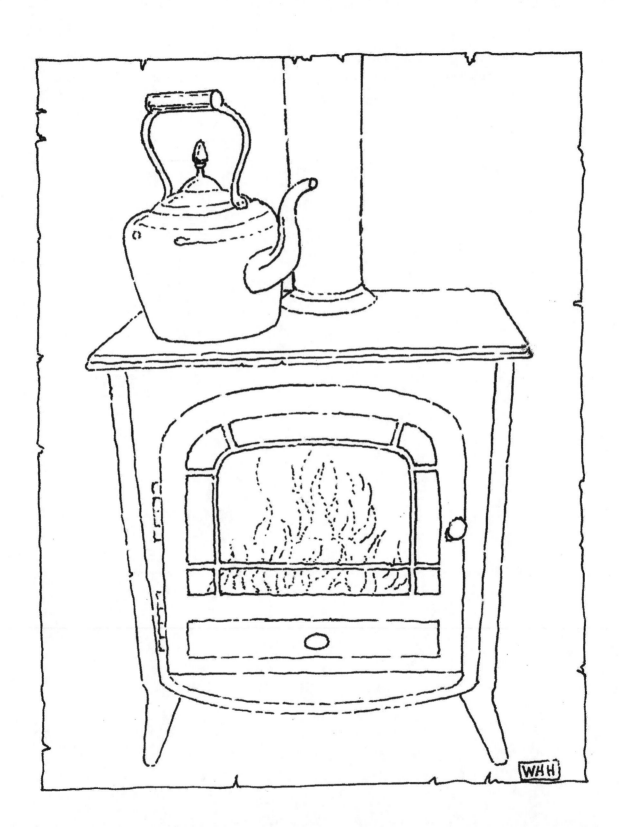

CHAPTER 24

Woodstove Cooking

Balanced, nutritious meals are important, especially if you live alone. It would be easy to slip into the habit of opening a can of vegetables and having that for dinner. I've done it. However I taught natural food cooking classes and I do know better. Not having electricity did rule out using my grain mill and my bread dough mixer.

I bought whole grain flour at the grocery or health food store and mixed up a simple flat bread dough that I fried in an iron skillet. Fast! The other bread I liked to make is bannock, which is like a biscuit cooked in a Dutch oven. We used to make it on our camping trips. It goes so well with breakfast, beans, or barbeque. Split the hot biscuit and spread it with jelly, honey, butter, or coconut oil and sprinkle with chia seeds and cinnamon.

It is difficult to keep butter fresh without refrigeration so I used olive oil. I also used coconut oil, which I call "the new butter." It doesn't require refrigeration either. Olive oil stays fresh longer than other oils. I had a can of herbes de Provence my sister had sent me and put those herbs in the oil. I like garlic in the oil and oregano or thyme, rosemary and dill mixtures. This is healthy and tastier than butter.

Having only a plastic ice chest for refrigeration, I managed to keep a few fresh vegetables. A block of ice took up a lot of room but that melted more slowly than cubes or crushed. I stopped by the general store several times a week for fresh ice on my way back from work. It's not necessary to keep root vegetables in the ice box if you are going to use them up within a week. Keep them in a metal bread box along with your bread to keep rodents away. Mice can demolish a loaf of bread in one night. Packrats will do their part, also. You will find that an assortment of tins, (metal lidded boxes) or canisters will come in very handy. Remember Grandma's cookie tins?

When cooking on a woodstove, it is important to remember that each stove is different. Mine was a small four-legged stove that opened in front with vents in the door, no burners on top, about twenty inches wide and thirty five inches deep. The chimney came out the top of the stove in the back. Considering all the things I used it for, it really worked hard. I have seen beautiful wood burning kitchen stoves with four burners, a side wood box, a compartment for hot water, and a warming shelf above to keep dishes warm until served.

Whichever kind of stove or fire pit you have, you must determine where hot, medium, and simmer are. There will be hot spots and cooler spots. If you are making soups or stews, find the hottest spot to bring water to a boil, add your ingredients, and move the pot toward the side or front to simmer. With a very hot fire the food will cook fast, so you have to plan which dish needs to cook the longest and which only needs a few minutes. I keep several long skewers on hand to place under a pot that needs to stay on the woodstove for several hours. These raise the pot up just a fraction of an inch and prevent scorching. Sometimes it is necessary to remove a pan from the stove for a bit. I kept an unsplit log standing on end next to the stove with an upside-down aluminum plate on top. It held any pot that needed to cool down a bit. All my pots, pans, and lids hung on the wall behind the woodstove. I left the stainless steel percolator coffee pot on the back of the stove always filled with water, ready for tea or hot chocolate. I didn't drink a lot of coffee.

It's good to make your stove work as efficiently as possible. Always do more than one thing when your stove is lit. If you are cooking breakfast, get the soup pot filled with water and heat it up for doing the dishes after breakfast. I left the big pot on the stove all night filled with water with the lid on. Even if the fire went out during the night, this gave me an extra head start in the morning. The water was still warm or hot and easy to pour or dip into the coffee pot. It might need only a little more heat to be ready for the dishes.

Dip some water out of the big pot into a saucepan for oatmeal. Hard boil some eggs in the big pot during breakfast for a snack or an egg salad sandwich later.

Living so far away from civilization I found I had to plan ahead before I went to town. I couldn't just run down to the corner. I would have had to drive past seven mountains to get to the "corner store."

Here are some of my favorite woodstove recipes:

HOMEMADE APPLESAUCE

1 bag of your favorite apples, about six pounds (If someone you know has a tree, ask if you can have the ones that drop to the ground if the deer don't get them first.)
About two cups of apple juice to start (This is a very casual recipe)

Wash the apples and cut out any bad spots. Quarter the apples and pull out the stems. Do not peel and do not cut out the cores. Place the cut apples in the soup kettle with the apple juice. Cover. Place the pot on the woodstove and allow apple juice to come to a boil. Move to a cooler spot and allow apples to simmer for an hour or more until all the apples are soft and are cooking in their own juices. Let the apples cool a little for ease of handling. Using a soup ladle, scoop out apples into a strainer sitting on a large pot or bowl. With a wooden spoon, mash the apples through the strainer, including as much of the skins as possible. At this time, if you wish, season with cinnamon, honey, nutmeg, cloves, or apple pie spice. Mixing this in while the apples are warm will get the flavors throughout the sauce and throughout the house. Bet it doesn't all make it into the refrigerator!

I prefer applesauce on my pancakes instead of syrup, unless it's real maple syrup. Don't have milk? I have also used cold applesauce on cold cereal when I have run out of milk. Mom taught us that as girls. She came through the Depression. It works.

A nice yogurt, applesauce, nut, and berry parfait makes a great breakfast. If you have raspberry or blackberry bushes on your land, this is where they will shine. Also, a cup of applesauce with a heaping tablespoon of bran or wheat germ mixed in "is good for what ails you." Lots of fiber. (Not for those who are gluten intolerant.)

DOUBLE CORN PANCAKES

1 cup whole wheat or white flour
1 cup corn meal
1 tsp. salt
2 tsp. baking powder
½ cup instant milk powder
2 cups corn, cut fresh from the cob, frozen, or canned, (drained)
2 cups buttermilk or two cups water (more as needed)
¼ cup honey

Mix all dry ingredients in large bowl. Stir in corn and milk/water, adding more water as needed. Add honey. Ladle a serving spoon full or two of batter onto a hot, oiled griddle on the woodstove. Turn when toasty on the bottom. Serve with butter if you have it or applesauce or yogurt and a sprinkle of cinnamon. A little honey or maple syrup is good.

HOT COCOA

¼ cup cocoa powder
½ tsp. salt
1 ½ cups instant milk powder
1 tsp. vanilla
¼ cup honey or ½ cup sugar
1 cup water

4 cups water, or leave out instant milk powder and substitute 4 cups milk (I use rice, coconut or almond milk in my recipe, and I realize this does not meet everyone's taste; however this is lactose free and non-mucus forming.)

In a 2-quart saucepan, add all the ingredients except the 4 cups water or milk. Using a wire whip or wooden spoon, mix all ingredients into the 1 cup of water. Set the pan on the woodstove and gradually add the water or milk. Slowly bring the cocoa mixture to just below boiling. Do not boil. With a soup ladle, dip out hot cocoa into cups and serve.

Admittedly, in a camping or backpacking situation, it is much easier to carry the small packets of hot chocolate mix.

MOUNTAIN TOAST

1 – 2 slices bread, Texas toast, whatever kind of bread you have
1 – 2 tbsp. butter per side, or oil if you don't have butter
Garlic powder or any favorite spice. Try cinnamon.

Melt butter in fry pan. Place bread on top of melted butter. Toast till light brown. Turn over, adding more butter, and sprinkle garlic powder on toasted side. Flip over briefly and sprinkle garlic powder on other side. Serve.

ACV WATER

1 soup spoon organic apple cider vinegar
12 to 16 ounces of water

Add apple cider vinegar to the water. This is thirst quenching and is rich in potassium. My bottle of ACV says it has 11 percent potassium. This is great if you've been outdoors splitting wood, sweating and need to replenish the electrolytes. It also settles my acid stomach. Farmers used to come in from the fields after plowing and make themselves a glass of ACV water.

C–WATER

This is not a recipe but it has come in handy to quench thirst and replace electrolytes. I carry packets of a vitamin C supplement called Emergen-C, which can not only quench thirst but restore vitamins and minerals with electrolytes. Open a packet and add to a glass of water. Great on hikes in a canteen.

HOMEMADE MAYONNAISE

1 egg
½ tsp. salt
½ tsp. mustard powder
2 tbsp. apple cider vinegar
1 cup olive oil, (or grape seed oil or avocado oil or mixture of both)

Place all ingredients in a tall medium bowl. If you have power, use a stick blender to blend all ingredients until thick. If the mayo breaks, add another egg and blend again. Since I had no electricity I used an old fashioned egg beater.

For a different flavor add garlic powder instead of mustard powder. Try sprinkling a small amount of dill in the mix or create your own signature blend with freshly ground pepper corns, cayenne pepper, or jalapeno.

CHAPATTIES (FLAT BREAD)

2 cups whole wheat flour
1 tsp. salt
any combination of herbs (see below)
¼ cup oil (olive oil works well)
1 cup water or more as needed

Mix together dry ingredients. Then add oil and water. Mix until a soft dough is formed. Turn out onto a floured board and knead about 10 times and form into five balls about 2-3 inches in diameter. Flatten with your hands, a rolling pin, or the side of a glass. Place in a hot, dry frying pan, cooking on one side for about 2 minutes and turn to the other side for another couple of minutes or so. Makes about 5 chapattis. Remove with a turner, place on a dinner plate and spread with butter, olive oil, or your favorite sandwich filling: a hot dog and mustard; peanut butter and jelly; a scoop of beans. If you aren't going to be using them right away, put them in a basket lined with a towel to keep them warm. If you only need to make one at a time, roll the rest in flour and place in a zipper bag and refrigerate. As you need more, remove from plastic bag, roll on a floured board or plate and cook in the pan as before.

Optional herbs: thyme and dill; rosemary; sesame seeds; turmeric; cayenne; cinnamon and honey; onion powder and dill. Get creative.

BANNOCK

2 cups buttermilk biscuit mix
½ cup dry 7-grain cereal
½ cup instant milk powder
2 tbsp. chia seeds
1 egg
2 tbsp. olive oil
1 cup water (Add more water if necessary)

Mix dry ingredients. Add egg, oil, and water. Mix dough gently. Do not knead. Divide into 7 or 8 balls of dough. On a floured board, gently pat into ½ inch thick biscuits, coating each with flour. Put 4 or 5 into the bottom of a hot ungreased Dutch oven. Cover and "bake" for 3 to 4 minutes. Remove cover, turn and "bake" with cover on for another 3 to 4 minutes. Altitude affects the length of cooking time. Check one inside to be sure they are done. Both sides should be toasty. Remove to plate, split, and butter. Whole grain goodness!

LENTIL SALAD

This salad is made with lentils you have sprouted yourself. Begin by measuring 1 cup of dried lentils into a quart jar. Fill jar with water. Allow to soak overnight. In the morning, pour off the water. (This water can be saved and used in soup or pancakes.) In the evening, pour more water into the jar just long enough to moisten the seeds. Pour off the water to use in other cooking. Rinse twice a day for two days. You should see tiny roots beginning to sprout from each lentil.

At this point, pour the sprouts into a medium-sized bowl. Chop up these additional ingredients and add to bowl:
2 medium/large tomatoes
½ large onion (or 1 medium)
1 large red bell pepper
⅓ cup green stuffed olives, sliced

If desired, you may add about two cups celery, chopped, and/or 1 medium cucumber, chopped
Use an Italian salad dressing or make up the dressing below. Pour into a cruet or an empty 16 oz. olive jar.
¼ cup water
3 tbsp. vinegar
a pinch of Kosher salt
¼ tsp. dill

dash oregano
½ tsp. thyme
½ tsp turmeric
¼ tsp. garlic powder

Pour the water and vinegar into the jar and shake. Add the herbs, spices, and salt. Shake again. Add ¾ cup olive oil. Shake well. Pour enough dressing over the tossed vegetables to coat well when mixed.

This is a hearty survival salad, enough to serve 4 to 5 people. Hot bread or bannock will go well with this dish and perhaps a bowl of plain yogurt with some fresh picked berries. Send the kids to find some before dinner under the "buddy" system along with one adult to supervise. Remember, bears love berries, too.

CHICKPEA SALAD

This is fast and simple, great with crackers and sliced apples.

In a medium bowl empty one drained can of chickpeas or any combination of mixed beans. Add the following:
1 large tomato, chopped
1 green bell pepper, chopped
Some chopped black olives
¼ small onion, chopped
¼ cup parsley or cilantro, chopped
½ small cucumber, chopped
lemon zest, if available
1 tbsp. pumpkin or sunflower seeds

Add Italian salad dressing or the homemade dressing above.

This has protein in the chickpeas/beans and five vegetables. For a hearty lunch or dinner, add sandwiches of homemade bread, peanut butter and jelly (or honey). If there are leftover baked beans, homemade or canned, put them between two slices of bread. Mom used to occasionally give us baked bean sandwiches during the War.

SALAD PLATTER

This is a fun lunch or dinner platter, depending on the ingredients you have on hand. I like to keep hard boiled eggs in the fridge or ice box. Start with a dinner plate that has been covered with romaine or other greens. Add some sunflower sprouts, radicchio, parsley, spinach, even chopped beet leaves and stems. On top of that place some cottage cheese, tomato wedges, egg wedges, cucumber slices, one or two artichoke hearts, a handful of frozen, defrosted peas, a pickle, a few green or black olives and a sprinkling of walnuts or sunflower seeds. Grate some lemon zest over all. Do this for each adult at the table. Children can have smaller portions.

Vinegar or lemon juice and olive oil dressing is good. Have some shaker jars of herbs on the table including coarse ground black pepper, cayenne pepper, turmeric, oregano, marjoram, dill, thyme, cumin, Italian herb mix, and so on. People can customize their salads.

Serve with whole grain crackers or a hearty bread.

COLE SLAW

This is a simple recipe of Mom's. I don't know if she realized how much I was watching. What she used to grate cabbage would be considered an antique now. Today I use a small Danish slicer which produces a hair thin slice about 1 inch long. Grate up half of a cabbage unless you have more than two people.

In a small bowl mix these ingredients:

2 heaping tablespoon of mayonnaise (see recipe above)

juice of ½ lemon

1 tsp. honey

2 tbsp. vinegar and oil dressing

1 tsp. lemon zest

Adjust amounts as desired

Add dressing to the grated cabbage. Cover and refrigerate immediately. Depending on the size of the cabbage this serves two to three.

ROAST BEEF AND VEGGIES

This recipe can be used with a beef roast, venison, or other wild-caught meat. Heat a large Dutch oven on the woodstove. When it is hot, sear the meat well in just a small amount of oil, first on one side and then on the other. This could take fifteen minutes or more. This is what gives the roast its deep, rich flavor. If you skip this step you will not have the results you want. Remove roast temporarily from stove. Cool a minute. Loosen the roast from the pan bottom. Add a cup or two of water. Watch out for the steam! Drop in a few beef bouillon cubes. Return pot to stove. Let the water return to a boil. Chop the following vegetables:

2 or 3 onions

8 carrots

4 potatoes, quartered

4 celery stalks
4 garlic cloves

Add the vegetables to the Dutch oven. Sprinkle herbs and spices over roast and vegetables:
oregano
thyme
salt and pepper
turmeric

Add 1 can of sliced mushrooms with liquid. Add more water to cover most of the vegetables. Lay about three rosemary sprigs over the top. Place cover on Dutch oven. To regulate heat better, place three or four long skewers under the Dutch oven. This raises the pot up enough to keep the roast from burning. Arrange the pan so the juices continue simmering for the rest of the day, about six hours. Check every hour to make sure liquid level does not get too low. If necessary, add more water. Taste gravy for flavor and add some minced garlic from a jar if necessary. Salt and pepper to taste.

Add more firewood as needed.

Pushing potatoes below the level of the gravy gives the potatoes a nice brown roasted color.

Depending on the size of the roast, this could serve five or six people.

BONE SOUP

Bone soup starts with a chicken, turkey, or other carcass. The nutrition and flavor comes from the bones but this can be enhanced with the addition of bouillon cubes. Leave the carcass in the same pot in which it was roasted. You'll be way ahead. Add about two cups water to the pan to deglaze the bottom. Let this simmer with the lid on for several hours, adding more water, until the bones are hot and dripping with juice and the meat starts to fall off the bones. If you have the time, add more water and allow the pot to sit on the woodstove for up to two days to draw out the marrow and the minerals in the bones. Use my tip of placing two long skewers under the pot to prevent scorching. Adding 1 – 2 tablespoons of vinegar also helps to draw out the minerals. Using tongs, lift out the bones and meat onto a large platter where they can continue dripping. Add two quarts water to pot. Add the following vegetables:
4 to 6 carrots sliced diagonally
3 onions, chopped
4 celery stalks, sliced diagonally
1 turnip, chopped
½ cup parsley, chopped
1 tsp. poultry seasoning (for chicken)
1 tsp. turmeric

salt and pepper to taste
½ cup white rice

Put lid back on the pan and bring to a simmer. While it is simmering, remove the meat from bones. Add ½ cup rice or more to pot and simmer for about 20 minutes, or according to package directions; brown rice takes about 50 minutes, again according to altitude. Test vegetables for doneness. Add meat and drippings in platter to pot and heat through. Taste test. In times when people had plenty of fire wood and the time, the bones were left simmering on the back of the stove for a couple of days. This was very nutritious. In survival times, time and ingredients might not be so generous.

This soup will serve about 6 people. Serve with sourdough bread and apple butter.

———————◆———————

Please keep in mind that I make no attempt to analyze amounts of protein, fats or carbohydrates in these recipes or the values of any foods. In a long-term survival situation we would be fortunate indeed to actually have all these ingredients on hand and we would need all the calories we could get.

CHAPTER 25

Saved by Seeds

About forty years ago, when I first started teaching my natural food cooking classes, I heard the story about a family during the great depression. Artistic license has been taken in order to bring this story into modern perspective.

This family was hungry because the husband had been out of work. They looked around to see what they could eat. They found some seeds they had put aside for the planting season—a bag of wheat, a sack of oats, some lentils, buckwheat, flax seeds, a container of dried peas, sunflower seeds, barley, and alfalfa seeds. They found some leftover packets of herb and vegetable seeds.

The mother and father mobilized the whole family. Children were given the chore of gathering all the old flower pots they had. They found some wooden flats and old buckets. They lined these up in the garage.

Next they washed all the canning jars from the previous season and set them aside. The girls cut out squares of cheesecloth, and found some elastic bands.

The boys dug some of the richest dirt they could find, filled buckets with it and filled all the flower pots with soil. In the buckets they planted a few tomato seeds and some cucumber and squash seeds. In the flower pots they planted different varieties of lettuce, parsley, spinach, and radishes. They put newspapers on the floor of the back enclosed porch, brought out cookie sheets and trays, and placed the freshly potted seeds on them.

The mother took canning jars, filled them almost full with water and added about a cup of dried lentils to one jar and a cup of wheat berries to another jar. She also added alfalfa and sunflower seeds to some of the jars. She covered the jars with cheesecloth and held it on with the elastic bands. She set the jars in a cabinet and let the seeds soak in the dark overnight. Then she put some lentils and barley into a soup pot with water to start making soup for the evening meal. Outside, she found some onions in the garden patch, a few late carrots, and one of the last leaves from the kale plant. Gathering a handful of dandelion greens from the yard, she added all of these to the soup pot. They would have dinner that night.

In the potato bin the father found some older potatoes that had grown long sprouts. He pulled out a trash can, hosed it out and filled it with more soil. He placed the potatoes down into the soil with the sprouted side up, covering each potato, but let the sprouts grow above the dirt. He moved the trash can to stand underneath one of the windows of the garage. The boys used the watering can to keep the soil moist in all the pots.

That evening, the family had lentil, barley, dandelion, vegetable soup seasoned with spices from the pantry. In the morning they had oatmeal sprinkled with cinnamon. After breakfast, the family took the jars of alfalfa and sunflower seeds, lentils, and wheat berries, from the cabinet and drained them. They placed them back in the cabinet until evening when they repeated the rinsing and draining. They saved all the rinse water and served it in small glasses to each family member. This water was rich in enzymes. They added any extra water to the watering can to water the vegetables. The rinse water speeded up the sprouting of the seeds in the pots. They also used the rinse water in soups and stews. The boys planted some of the dried peas in the wooden flats, then moved them to the fence so the vines would be supported.

The sprouting seeds grew each day, providing a variety of tiny greens for salads and soup. After only two days, the lentils showed tiny roots growing and the wheat berries were putting out sprouts. These sprouts could be eaten at this point or allowed another day or so to be ready for a salad. As seeds sprouted, their nutritional value increased many times. The life force was released and at this point the highest nutritional value was available.

The family continued working their plan. It took only a few days before the lettuce, spinach, parsley, and radishes sprouted in the pots with the sun warming the soil on the porch. Soon the tomato and cucumber plants spread their leaves, put out buds and flowers and then the fruit. The peas in the flats grew, put out leaves, and began the climb up the fence. As one crop grew and was harvested, the flats were replanted with buckwheat seeds, allowed to grow until the plants were six to eight inches high, cut off at ground level and used as lettuce substitutes in salads and sandwiches. This process only took a week. Fresh soil was added as needed for the next planting.

The family survived for six months using this system with just leftover seeds and grains. The husband finally found a job and was able to bring home more food. However, the family did not abandon the system using sprouted seeds and taught the children they could survive very well working together using what they had.

Today we have such a great variety of seeds available that can be bought in one-pound packages.

Seeds are the beginning of things. They have the power of life within them. Just add water. The water saturates the seed. Strange chemical changes begin to happen as the seed swells. The inside starts to push out. The shell of the seed is too small, too confining. The dormant life within the heart of the seed knows it's time. The water inside the seed has mixed together phytochemicals, acids, minerals, readying the seed for heat. Photosynthesis. The photons from the sun quickly warm the seed, energizing it. Pop! There is a little nose of a root pushing down into the soil. Pop! Here is a shoot pushing up toward the sun. The hidden energy inside the seed is released. The shoot turns green. The nutrients from the soil add to the energy in the seed and there is no stopping it. As God planned, man has planted it, the rains have watered it, and God has brought the increase. That is food for the hungry soul—out of a seed.

Most people have tasted alfalfa, clover, and radish sprouts. It is fairly easy to grow sprouts in a quart jar. Sprouts can be grown in jars in any kitchen, apartment, condominium, mobile home, motor home, trailer, tent, or tree house. After the sprouts have been growing for three to six or seven days, rinsed twice a day, they can be removed from the jars and placed into plastic zipper bags and put into backpacks or in the fridge for salad and sandwiches over the next few days.

Ann Wigmore used to travel with her wheat sprouts in jars. She was the nutritionist who started the Hippocrates diet years ago. She and a doctor friend discovered that by adding a small amount of wheat grass juice to a glass of tap water, toxins were neutralized along with fluoride (*The Wheatgrass Book* by Ann Wigmore, pg. 62).

It is possible to grow your own wheat grass in a flat containing potting soil. This would require a stable living situation where you would not be mobile and where you would have a good surface or shelf to hold the flats while the wheat grass grows eight inches high. At that time the entire tray of grass can be harvested (cut at dirt level), immediately put into a large zipper bag or a quart jar, and refrigerated. Then, as needed, remove a handful, put it through a wheat grass juicer, or snip with scissors onto a salad, providing vitamins and minerals for the day. Snipped wheatgrass can also be added to your green juice drinks made with the new bullet-type blenders. This is live food and an inexpensive substitute for buying supplements. For more information on sprouting you can go to Hippocrates Health Institute Greenhouse, and watch Michael, the wheatgrass expert. I have seen many of his DVDs.

You may have all sorts of dried foods, rice, varieties of pasta, dehydrated vegetables, various seasonings—all well and good. However, in tough times you will not be able to go out and buy vitamins, supplements, and energizing drinks to keep yourself healthy and strong. This is where sprouts shine. Practice now, learning the simple art of sprouting alfalfa seeds for sandwiches, growing wheat grass and harvesting it to snip into your salads, or juicing it. Stand a few sprigs of wheat grass or mint in your glass of water. Sprout some lentils for two or three days. Just remember not to throw out the soaking water. This water is rich in vitamins and enzymes. You can dilute it half and half in water and drink it, according to Ann Wigmore as mentioned above, who is the mother of the sprouting movement in America. Water your plants with it and watch them put out new growth. Make the lentil salad in the chapter on woodstove cooking. It takes just five ingredients plus homemade salad dressing served on a bed of alfalfa sprouts or buckwheat sprouts. Fill your meals with homegrown vitamins and minerals. Practice now and hard times won't seem so hard.

Seeds are an incredible wealth to the home gardener. For generations the "dooryard garden" has been the traditional place to grow small crops of fresh herbs, flowers, lettuce, collards, Swiss chard, tomatoes, cucumbers, mint, and edible flowers like nasturtium flowers and leaves. Gardeners grew honeysuckle, rose hips, periwinkle vines, and flax to make linen fabric for tablecloths, napkins, and dish towels. Fall crops such as spinach, Brussels sprouts, kale, and cabbage bring hearty nutrition into the winter home. Cabbage in the form of sauerkraut and other fermented vegetables, such as radishes, beets, celery root, carrots, Swiss chard stems, and turnips, all add nutrition and flavor made in crocks without refrigeration.

I just purchased an excellent book on fermentation, *Real Food Fermentation* by Alex Lewin, detailing step-by-step instructions on how to ferment vegetables and make yogurt and kefir.

When the children were young, I used to make yogurt in quart jars in a warm water bath in a roasting pan in my gas oven overnight, letting the gas pilot light maintain the heat on low. The next morning, I refrigerated the quarts of fresh yogurt except one, which was served on hot oatmeal or pancakes. I liked yogurt on crackers or toast. Later I tried kefir. It turned out quite well. I also made fresh whole wheat bread every week, grinding the grain, kneading, forming loaves, and bringing hot bread out of the oven in just a couple of hours. The same dough made the best honey nut rolls and apple-walnut-coconut braid. Great memories.

In a sprouting kitchen, you will need some glass jars, preferably quart size, to give the sprouts room to grow. If cheesecloth is not available, squares of clean pantyhose work very well, allowing the water to be drained after each rinse and let air circulate. Elastic bands do the best job of holding the fabric on the jars. I have found it easiest to pick up a case of jars for food storage each time I do large grocery shopping. Remember, in hard times plastic wrap, plastic storage containers, plastic storage bags won't be available. Small jelly jars or pint jars will come in handy for food storage and they are reusable and can be sterilized. Remember Grandma's glass, stackable, lidded refrigerator jars? You might just find some of these at a recycle shop.

Pick up one or two gallons of plain white vinegar. Vinegar can be used as a disinfectant as it kills germs and bacteria. Put half a cup of vinegar in a bowl of water and keep it near your sink to wash off the vegetables before they are used or put half and half vinegar and water into a spray bottle to spray the vegetables. (Think about how many people have handled that avocado before you picked it up.) This same vinegar can be used as a natural deodorant, a spray to clean up around the sink, as a disinfectant to clean or mop up floors, and to clean windows. I got a tip about using a mixture of one gallon white vinegar with one cup dish detergent and two cups Epsom salts to kill weeds on the sidewalk and driveway.

Another use for vinegar is to polish copper pots. I still have the copper-bottomed pots from years ago. After cleaning a pot, I spray some vinegar onto the copper bottom and shake on some salt. You can see the shining action start immediately. Rub this over the copper until it's evenly shiny. Rinse and dry right away.

Something to consider in a survival kitchen is a solar generator. These generators can be kept in a cabinet or under the kitchen table, somewhere out of the way. I have a special, custom fifty foot Anderson cord which came with my generator that will reach from the kitchen corner out the door (or a window) to my solar panel next to the porch facing the sun. It uses no fuel, has no odor or fumes, is quiet, and is ready to work whenever the power goes out. It's heavy, so I keep mine on a small dolly that I found at a tool shop. There is a leash tied to the front so I can move it around the house as needed. These generators can power small kitchen tools like beaters, mixers, and lights, recharge cell phones, and keep the refrigerator going. This will not work for electric stoves. Your radio will run, keeping you informed about weather and other events. Be very thankful for the good of the earth and everything you have.

So, enjoy your freshly sprouted salad tonight knowing you grew it yourself. Your children will also be more likely to eat anything they helped to grow. Remember, we serve a God who promises to supply all our needs, according to His riches in glory through Christ Jesus.

Listen, if I can live alone in my mid to late sixties, on the side of a rugged mountain at ninety five hundred feet, then, maybe you can, too, at a lower altitude right where you are. And my pilgrimage was more than fifteen years ago. I may seem old to you now, but I have been taught well by many people down through the years. Now I have been able to pass it on to you. I hope with all my heart this encourages you, and, to quote Winston Churchill, whom I remember hearing tell his countrymen decades ago: "Never, never, never, give up!" I wonder what George Washington and the rest of our founding fathers would say to us today. The same thing they said in 1776! "Give us liberty or give us death!"

EPILOGUE

As I stand here on my mountain a few years later, I think back to all I've learned, all that the land itself has taught me. To have survived is one thing but to have had the land love me back to health and joy, to have it show me its beauty in its wildest way, to allow its strength to seep into my bones, to drench me with its dew and to teach me to stand as tall as the trees, to be as firm in my faith as the rocks and to stand on the rock of my salvation, to trust Him, the King of kings! This is my victory.

How magnificent it is to sit in the evenings pondering how huge the universe is, to watch the sun end a perfect day, or walk quietly among God's beautiful trees, thanking Him for their shade and shelter, their firewood and their bounty! I listen to the wind whispering and soughing through the pines, that comforting sound that puts me to sleep at night. The clouds float over the distant valley, glowing in the sunset, and the Blood of Christ Mountains shine red in the sunrise. The smoke of past Indian campfires and women grinding grain in their stone mills along with the voices of future children building tree houses on the slopes all mingle together to form what is Peace Mountain.

I walk around my place now, seeing the new well, just put in a short time ago. There is so much water here. The trees know it. They thrive. The winter snows have seeped deep into the earth, down, down to the underground streams, down to the aquifer that will quench our thirst for years to come. The log cabin will go up right over there in the middle of that stand of trees I call The Cathedral. The shoulder of the mountain will shelter it from the harsh winds that come from the north from time to time. Soon I will be cooking a fragrant meal, simple but hearty, a roast with herbs of rosemary, thyme, garlic, lots of carrots, onions, potatoes, in my new kitchen, my copper pots hanging from the beam overhead, Mom's old oil lamp hanging over the table, fresh, hot bread on the board. After dinner we'll sit out on the deck that wraps itself around the house, quietly watching the deer.

They come in the early evenings, browsing slowly through the glen just as they have for hundreds of years, each generation teaching the next: "Here man is friendly. You can be safe here. Sometimes they put out corn for us, and sometimes they plant lettuce among the trees for us to nibble. And there is always a tub of clean water for us to drink."

Later we will go back inside to warm ourselves by the fire, to have a gentle conversation about the accomplishments of the day, to be thankful for my sons who have been strong arrows in my quiver, who have been there to "contend with our enemies in the gates." And we have won many battles together and created tales to tell.

I remember driving back up into the high valley early one evening with an upslope condition moving into the area. As I topped the last rise, I saw the first tendrils of a delicate mist pouring over the hills, coming down through the draws like a giant waterfall, effervescent sparkling wisps catching the rays of the tangerine sun, slowly sinking into the valley, like a down-filled comforter, losing some of its feathers.

I had to pull over and watch this amazing sight. God had stopped the clock for me to experience this slow, easy, lovely nightfall. Had I gotten home sooner I would have missed this simple splendor. I stood there, feeling the moisture of the mists surround me, breathing in the fresh vapor, reflecting the orange and red of the setting sun. As it drifted past me quickly, I realized it would soon be dark and I needed to get home to my warm woodstove and my books. Next to the woodstove would be the neatly split logs stacked there by my youngest son, Josh, on a brief visit, and more in the next room in reserve for a long, cold night. Thank you, son.

They say you can't take anything with you when you die. They are wrong. For years I have been an in-home caregiver and I have taken care of many older people who are at the end of their lives. They are the ones who ask the really tough questions. They don't bother with the younger generation's questions such as "Is there a God?" or "How did the universe begin?" No, they ask, "What's it like to die?" "Does God love me?" "Will I go to heaven?" "Who will be there?" "Will my pets be there?" "Will my friends recognize me?" "Will my parents be there, my sisters and brothers?" "Has God forgiven my sins?" Oh boy!

I remember one of the ladies I had taken care of asking me what heaven is like. I told her I couldn't say experientially, but from everything I had studied and heard it was a beautiful place, full of light and hope. Jesus would be there waiting for her at the gates and her husband would be waiting to show her all the trees he planted along the rivers and streams. She commented that "you can't take anything with you." I reminded her of all the special memories she would take with her of her life, her home, her children and friends, and that she would recognize all of them and they would greet her. I sensed she asked these questions because she knew her time was short. A few weeks later she died quietly and gently in my arms and melted safely into the care of her Savior, Jesus.

No, I can't take my land with me but I have my Lord, who will never leave me nor forsake me. I have my memories of the years I've spent here on my wild mountain. I have the memories of the friends and neighbors who have helped me, taught me, given me water to drink. Their reward will be very great in heaven. I will remember the laughter between friends, the sharing of meals, the horses we rode through the hills, effortlessly climbing steep slopes and down dry draws. I will remember the gold of my aspen trees in the fall, the rain on my tin roof, the lowing of the cattle as they browsed and rested, chewing their cud in the afternoons outside my windows. I will remember the nuthatches in the woodpile teaching their young about life, the freezing mists at night, the hail, the time I almost froze in my bed.

And long after I'm gone, each generation will come to the glen looking for peace here on this mountain as I have. They will sit on the deck in the evenings, waiting for God to speak to them also. The birds and the bears will come; the coyotes will still chase the rabbits; the owl will fly through the glen, hoping for an early dinner; the wildcats will still steal cat food out of the barns; and the catamount, the mountain lion, will prowl as he always has as the king of the beasts. The sun will rise and set. The mists will fill the valley. The moon will move through its phases and give us its warnings of white and red. The cry of the golden eagle, as he catches an updraft, will echo between the hills. Evening and morning, spring time and harvest will not end until that day when Gabriel will blow the great shofar and Yehshua/Jesus, the Commander of the Armies of the Living God, will split the skies, call our names and lead us home.

AMEN

HELPFUL WEBSITES

www.TheSilverEdge.com Toll free calling: 1-888-528-0559, fax: 1602-943-2363
Micro-Particle Colloidal Silver Generator, $349. 95 plus S&H. (also silver wire)
Verification Code: PILGRIM

www.HeirloomSolutions.com Toll free calling: 1-800-280-3465
Heirloom seeds and Catalogue, non-hybrid seeds, bulk pricing, Heirloom Seed Banks

info@solutionsfromscience.com 1-877-327-0365
Solar generators and other solar products, chia seeds, other survivor items
Solutions from Science
2200 Illinois Route 84
P.O. Box 518
Thompson, Il 61285

www.jimbakkershow.com
Bulk food, solar generators, water filters/pitchers, 12 volt blankets, more